KT-441-548

EAST SUSSEX
WITHDRAWN
11 JUN 2024
19

04447346

Energy Balls
& Power Bites

Energy Balls
& Power Bites

all-natural snacks for healthy energy boosts

Sara Lewis

PHOTOGRAPHY BY WILLIAM SHAW

LORENZ BOOKS

This edition is published by Lorenz Books, an imprint of Anness Publishing Ltd, 108 Great Russell Street, London WC1B 3NA; info@anness.com

www.lorenzbooks.com; www.annesspublishing.com; twitter: @Anness_Books

If you like the images in this book and would like to investigate using them for publishing, promotions or advertising, please visit our website www.practicalpictures.com for more information.

© Anness Publishing Ltd 2017

All rights reserved. No part of this publication may be reproduced, stored in a retrieval system, or transmitted in any way or by any means, electronic, mechanical, photocopying, recording or otherwise, without the prior written permission of the copyright holder.

A CIP catalogue record for this book is available from the British Library.

Publisher: Joanna Lorenz
Photography: William Shaw
Food for photography: Sara Lewis
Nutritional consultant: Joy Skipper
Designer: Adelle Mahoney
Styling: Pene Parker
Editorial: Sarah Lumby

PUBLISHER'S NOTE
Although the advice and information in this book is believed to be accurate and true at the time of going to press, neither the author nor the publisher can accept any legal responsibility or liability for any errors or omissions that may have been made, nor for any inaccuracies nor for any loss, harm or injury that comes about from following instructions or advice in this book.

With thanks to Magimix for the loan of the food processors used in the step by step pictures.

COOK'S NOTES
Bracketed terms are intended for American readers. For all recipes, quantities are given in both metric and imperial measures and, where appropriate, in standard cups and spoons. Follow one set of measures, but not a mixture, because they are not interchangeable.
Standard spoon and cup measures are level.
1 tsp = 5ml, 1 tbsp = 15ml, 1 cup = 250ml/8fl oz.
Australian standard tablespoons are 20ml. Australian readers should use 3 tsp in place of 1 tbsp for measuring small quantities.
American pints are 16fl oz/2 cups. American readers should use 20fl oz/2.5 cups in place of 1 pint when measuring liquids.
Electric oven temperatures in this book are for conventional ovens. When using a fan oven, the temperature will probably need to be reduced by about 10–20°C/20–40°F. Since ovens vary, you should check with your manufacturer's instruction book for guidance.
The nutritional analysis given for each recipe is calculated per portion (i.e. serving or item), unless otherwise stated. If the recipe gives a range, such as Serves 4–6, then the nutritional analysis will be for the smaller portion size, i.e. 6 servings. The analysis does not include optional ingredients, such as salt added to taste.
Medium (US large) eggs are used unless otherwise stated.

Contents

Introduction

Are there moments in the day when you lack energy, and need a boost to keep you alert? Our bodies need power to carry out all the normal bodily functions we take for granted every hour of every day – walking to work, going to the gym, shopping, eating, and even just sitting and reading a book. Without energy even our brains would struggle to function. For children this need is even higher as their bodies are constantly growing and they too lead very busy lives.

Keeping energy levels up doesn't mean reaching for a processed snack or sweet. While we may crave a cookie as a mid-morning or mid-afternoon snack, it might give a quick energy boost but that is soon over. This kind of snacking adds sugar without you even really noticing. The amount of sugar that we consume has come under close scrutiny and is now thought to be more of a problem than the amounts of fat that we eat.

All the recipes in this book are made with reduced sugar, adding sweetness instead from natural fruits and vegetables that also provide complex carbohydrates, vitamins and minerals to help you to function and perform at an optimum level. Wholegrains, nuts and seeds provide the base, and many recipes are given an extra boost with spirulina, soya, hemp and pea protein powders, to super-power those who are trying to get fit, or for those trying to cut down on meat and dairy.

There are snacks that can be made in just a matter of minutes, to those that can be made ahead and kept in the fridge or freezer ready to grab and go. Fight the fatigue with these fantastic pick-you-up energy balls, bites, clusters, bars and snacks that are not just tasty but healthy too.

Above, clockwise from top: Super-powered spirulina balls p66, gingered beet & blackberry balls p78, very berry energy balls p84, apricot & coconut balls, p86, dark chocolate super-booster p64, minted matcha & almond balls p76.

Controlling blood sugar

If you feel that you are lacking in energy and concentration this could be down to unbalanced blood sugar levels. Glucose is a sugar needed by all the cells in the body to function (especially the brain cells), and it's important that the concentration of glucose in the blood is maintained at a constant level. When you eat a meal, particularly one that is high in carbohydrates such as pasta, bread and cakes, the level of glucose in your blood rises. Insulin is pumped into your system and as a response, glucose is stored in the cells for future use as glycogen. But the body can only store a certain amount, and if you don't burn off excess glucose in the body it will turn to fat – which is why we need to focus on sugar rather than fat when trying to fight obesity.

Above: Make a chocolate cake with naturally sweet beetroot (see p136) so you can cut down on the refined sugar but retain the flavour.

Opposite, top: Apples are rich in energy-boosting fruit sugars, a better alternative for snacking. Here they are dried into delicious crisps.

Opposite, centre: Almonds, cacao and dried cranberries are excellent nutrient-filled ingredients for energy snacks.

Opposite, bottom: Grains, nuts, seeds, frozen berries, yogurt and mint leaves can be whizzed up into energy balls in minutes.

On the flipside, if you don't eat for a long time, the blood sugar can fall too low, which is when your energy stores start to run out (it's a bit like asking your car to move when you've not put any fuel into it), and this is when you may suffer fatigue, lethargy or even dizzy spells, and are very likely to reach for the nearest pick-me-up – normally a caffeine-laden coffee or sugar-laden treat.

If you plan your daily eating habits correctly, you won't have an afternoon slump, or reach for the biscuit tin or a shot of caffeine to keep you alert, awake and functioning well. Starting the day with a good breakfast is important for a lot of people, bearing in mind it's probably been over 10 hours since you ate dinner the night before, so blood-sugar level is low at this time. Planning ahead to have time for breakfast is the best option, but if you don't have the spare minutes for breakfast at home, take one of the delicious muesli bars (pages 100–121) to eat on your journey to school or work.

Throughout the day think about eating little and often – around every 3 hours – so that your blood sugar remains at a constant level, without the dips and highs. Including protein and fat in every meal and snack is also helpful in blood-sugar control, and will also be more satiating, meaning you eat less in the long run.

HOW DOES YOUR BODY MAKE ENERGY?
Energy comes from the food we eat – our bodies digest the food by breaking it down with enzymes and other important molecules, starting with the saliva in our mouths down to the stomach that is rich with stomach acid. Carbohydrates (which are simply sugars and starches) are broken down into another type of sugar, known as glucose; proteins and fats also provide energy but this process takes a bit longer to work. To enable the energy system to function a lot of other nutrients are required – B vitamins, magnesium, manganese, amino acids and fatty acids – so a varied diet is hugely important to ensure you are getting all of these. And most importantly, none of this can happen without oxygen and water! So taking exercise and making sure you are never dehydrated is key to building up your energy levels.

BOOSTING CONCENTRATION
The brain does use glucose to function, and needs a constant supply; studies have shown that dips in glucose availability can have a negative impact on attention, learning and memory. So sending your child off to school with no breakfast really can affect how they perform in class. Two thirds of our daily intake of glucose is needed by the brain, as it is constantly active, even when we are asleep, and it competes with the rest of the body for glucose when levels dip very low, another reason for maintaining a balanced level of blood sugar at all times. The recipes for balls and bites in this book have been created so that you can control your intake of glucose throughout your day.

Reducing sugar

Sugar has been a lifelong treat for most of us, but now we are putting our health at risk by over-consuming this addictive ingredient. The World Health Organization recommends that adults get no more than 5% of their calories from refined sugar, which is about 6 teaspoons. The National Diet and Nutrition Survey estimates that people in the UK consume around 15 teaspoons of sugar per day, whilst in the US the total is around 46 teaspoons – that is a lot of sugar!

Research indicates quite clearly that sugar has an addictive quality. Sugar is known as an anti-nutrient – to enable the body to process it, other nutrients must be used, and this could mean a deficiency in some important nutrients – but sugar itself provides empty calories, with no nutritional value at all. It's important to stress that this refers to the refined sugar added to your food and drink and not the naturally occurring sugar in foods such as fruits, vegetables and grains. But as we should be getting enough sugar from natural foods anyway, additional sugar isn't usually necessary in our diets.

For years we were told to reduce the fat in our diets, and we turned to low-fat products, most of which contained a huge amount of added sugar, and over time our bodies have become de-sensitised to sugar and we crave even more. Eating too much sugar which is not burned off can lead to weight gain, which in turn increases the risk of health conditions such as heart disease and type 2 diabetes.

Luckily it is possible to wean yourself off sugar and to learn how to eat real nutritious food rather than empty calories. Reducing sugar intake can be done gradually. Each day cut down on the amount you add to your drinks, and swap your morning biscuit

Below: Raw cane sugar crystals are made from pure sugar cane juice that is evaporated. The crystals are high in minerals and are low on the glycaemic index.

with one of the protein-rich healthy energy balls in this book. Eating good protein and fat will help to wean yourself off sugar. Aim for small steps over two to three months and you'll be amazed at how quickly you get used to less sugar.

UNDERSTANDING SUGAR

Sugar is a collective term used for any soluble sweet-tasting carbohydrate. Generally the different kinds end in -ose: glucose is found in all carbohydrates, this is the form the body uses for energy; sucrose is made from sugar beet or cane; fructose is a fruit sugar found in fruits and vegetables; lactose is a milk sugar found in milk products; maltose is made from grains; and dextrose is also made from grains. The chemical composition of the various different types of sugar affects how the body absorbs them, how they affect your metabolism, and what they do to your appetite.

NATURAL SWEETNESS

Where possible it is always preferable to rely on the natural sweetness of foods rather than having to add sugar or artificial sweeteners. Mixing naturally sweet fruit or vegetables into cakes and muesli bars means that you can greatly reduce the amount of refined sugar that you would normally add.

Fruit and vegetables not only add sweetness, they are also rich in vitamins, minerals and much-needed fibre for our diets. A lot of the recipes in this book use dates, figs and bananas (although, dried fruits are very high in sugar so be wary of eating these too often) as well as vegetables such as carrots, beetroot and sweet potatoes. Sometimes adding spices can also help in giving a 'sweet' taste – cinnamon and vanilla are good for this, plus cinnamon is also effective in controlling blood sugar and reducing the risk for developing type 2 diabetes, so this spice is doubly useful! So what are the alternatives instead of sugar? Here and on the next pages are a few of the 'natural' options available.

Above: Coconut crystals are the evaporated ground form of coconut nectar. They are both rich in antioxidants, iron, zinc, calcium and potassium, and about three-quarters as sweet as sugar. **Below:** If you search out raw, unpasteurised honey from organic farms it is a healthy, natural food in moderation.

Sweet alternatives

A range of natural and unprocessed sweeteners are available; they can vary in quality from one brand to the next, so select with care when purchasing.

STEVIA
Stevia comes from the leaves of the South American stevia plant, and although a recent addition in the West has been used for over 40 years in Japan. Make sure the stevia you buy is pure stevia, as some products contain dextrose and flavourings. It can have a slightly bitter aftertaste.

Below, from left to right:
In the absence of sugar give your energy snacks a sweet taste with ground cinnamon, cinnamon sticks, a vanilla pod (bean) and vanilla extract.

AGAVE
From the agave plant in Mexico, the sap is boiled to produce the sweet syrup. Some commercially-produced agave is made from the starch of the root bulb and the final product is very high in fructose, so try to find the syrup that has been produced in the traditional way. Look for raw agave nectar, which is minimally processed and with a thick gel-like texture. It has a steadying effect on blood sugar and also acts as a prebiotic. Agave nectar and agave syrup are the same thing.

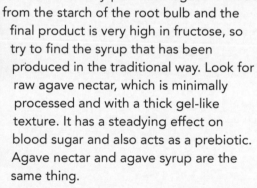

HONEY
Although a very natural ingredient, honey is still classed as a simple sugar and is absorbed into the bloodstream quickly, giving a sugar spike, which is not good if you are trying to control your blood sugar or to lose weight. If you do use honey then avoid blended honeys as they are often heated which means their natural goodness is destroyed. Also be aware that commercial beekeepers may also feed sugar or high-

fructose corn syrup to their bees (because it is cheap!), so you are not getting 'natural' sweetness. Try only to use organic and use sparingly. Omit honey from recipes if following a vegan diet and substitute maple syrup.

Above, from left to right: Stevia, agave, honey, maple syrup and molasses are alternatives to refined sugar.

MAPLE SYRUP

Made from the sap of maple trees this syrup contains both antioxidant and anti-inflammatory properties. It also causes the least problems with regards to digestion so is usually recommend for people who suffer with IBS. It contains zinc, magnesium and calcium. Be sure to buy maple syrup and not maple-flavoured syrup, which does not include all these great qualities – pay a little more to get the real thing.

MOLASSES

Also called black treacle and blackstrap molasses, this is the by-product of the process used to extract sugar from sugar cane. Molasses is a good source of vitamin B6, magnesium, manganese and potassium.

Vegetarians often eat molasses as a source of iron, but search out organic molasses as pesticide traces can be found. Molasses has a strong flavour so a little goes a long way.

What does protein do?

Proteins are large, complex molecules that play many crucial roles in the body – they are not just for beefy muscles! Proteins do most of the work required for the structure, function and regulation of the body's tissue and organs, and are used as a source of fuel when glycogen levels are low. They also produce antibodies to help protect the body from viruses and bacteria, and produce enzymes to carry out chemical reactions that take place in cells, plus they assist with the formation of new molecules by reading the genetic information stored in DNA. Proteins help bind and carry atoms, and there are also messenger proteins used for signals and biological processes between cells, tissues and organs.

We can get protein from a number of foods, such as lean meat, poultry, fish, eggs, pulses and legumes, nuts and seeds. But sometimes we need an extra boost, maybe after training or after a race – muscle tissue proteins are continually being broken down during exercise and additional protein is needed to compensate for this, and to facilitate repair and growth. The greater the exercise intensity and the longer the duration of the exercise, the more protein is being used. The recipes in this book contain lots of protein-rich nuts, seeds and supplement powders, especially those from the power balls chapter (p62–99), perfect for after-gym snacks.

Opposite, from top: Almonds, cashew nuts, pumpkin seeds and hulled hemp seeds.

Below, left to right: Chia seeds, nuts and quinoa flakes are all useful for adding protein to your energy snacks.

Nut and seed power

Nuts provide most of the B vitamins and
the minerals phosphorous, iron, copper and
potassium. Many raw nuts, especially almonds,
are also a rich source of vitamin E, although both vitamin E
and thiamine are destroyed when nuts are roasted. Almonds
are thought to lower cholesterol, are low in saturated fatty
acids, are rich in unsaturated fatty acids, and contain fibre,
calcium, phytosterol antioxidants as well as plant protein.
Cashew nuts have a lower fat content than most other nuts,
and contain heart-healthy mono-unsaturated fats, similar to
those found in olive oil. Selenium can be a difficult mineral for
someone on a vegan diet to obtain and brazil nuts are an
excellent source of selenium; just one nut can give you a day's
supply. Walnuts are rich in omega-3 essential fatty acids
which are vital for normal tissue growth and development.

Seeds are cheap and easy to buy, and add extra nutritional
value to any muesli bar or power ball. Pumpkin seeds contain
iron for healthy blood, magnesium for maintaining healthy
body cells, and zinc for normal growth and
development. Chia seeds add protein, fibre, omega 3,
6 and 9 fatty acids plus calcium, iron, copper and
zinc. Hemp is rich in essential fatty acids with two
thirds of omega 6 and one third omega 3 fatty
acids, and contains 21 known amino acids,
including the 9 essential amino acids, the
building blocks of protein, as well as B
vitamins, vitamin E, carotene, calcium and
magnesium. Buy hemp as hulled seeds, as these are
easier for the body to digest and extract the important
nutrients, or as oil, or as a fine green powder. Flaxseeds,
also called linseeds, can be bought as brown or
golden seeds. When ground they are one of
the best food sources of lignans, which are
rich in antioxidants and act as
phytoestrogens, which help balance
hormone levels.

Protein supplements

Above: Hemp powder is an ingredient that can be easily blended into your power balls to increase the protein content.

Protein supplements are not a substitute for a poor diet, but if you have particularly high protein requirements they may be a convenient way to make up the shortfall, and are perfect for adding a boost to some of the energy snacks in this book.

WHEY PROTEIN
Extracted from curdled milk, isolated whey protein has a higher bio-availability (percentage of protein that is retained and used in the body for repair and growth) than any wholefood source – it has a profile that is better matched to muscle protein than any other food. It is also very easy to digest. Whey minimises muscle protein breakdown during high-intensity exercise. It also includes immune-enhancing capabilities as it includes antioxidants. This may be the best type of protein to have immediately after training (assuming you don't have any dairy dietary restrictions).

CASEIN
Casein travels through the gut more slowly than whey protein, which may help it to be absorbed in greater quantities. Your daily schedule will dictate how useful this is – it could be beneficial to take in the evening, or when you know you will not be eating for several hours. It also has a higher bio-availability than most foods.

SOYA PROTEIN
Soya protein has the highest concentration of the key amino acids (building blocks for protein) that are important for muscle growth, which makes it a good protein to include during intense exercise. It may also enhance the production of thyroid hormones, which are important for regulating the metabolic rate.

PEA PROTEIN

Pea protein comes from yellow peas and it contains all the essential amino acids. It is also allergen-free, making it good for those that cannot digest whey, but the research behind it is not as strong as that for soya and whey.

HEMP POWDER

Hemp is a great choice for those following a vegan diet as it is also rich in omega-3 and omega-6 fatty acids. It is richer in dietary fibre than most other protein powders.

EGG PROTEIN

Egg protein has a higher bio-availability than any wholefood source, but not as high as whey isolates.

Below, clockwise from top right: Pea protein, soya protein, whey protein and hemp powder.

Good carbohydrates

Below, from top to bottom right: Quinoa flakes, rye flakes, buckwheat flakes and porridge (rolled) oats.

Carbohydrates often get a bad press, however we need them for energy rather like a car needs fuel to run. Carbohydrates come in two forms, simple and complex (or simple sugars and starches), the difference being their chemical structure and also how quickly they are digested and absorbed.

Simple carbohydrates are made of just one or two sugar molecules, and are the quickest source of energy as they are very rapidly digested. These include table sugar, honey, jam and fizzy drinks, and are likely to leave you feeling hungry and craving more just after you've eaten them.

Complex carbohydrates are made up of a chain of sugar molecules and are often rich in fibre, so are more satisfying and healthy as they take longer to break down and therefore give you lasting energy. They are also more likely to be rich in vitamins and minerals, and include foods such as colourful vegetables and wholegrains. Lots of the recipes in this book include grains such as oats, quinoa, buckwheat flakes and rye: good carbohydrates that are useful for long-term energy.

OATYLICIOUS
Porridge (rolled) oats, compared with other grains, have one of the highest concentrations of protein, minerals, B vitamins and vitamin E. Plus they are an important source of soluble and insoluble fibre. The soluble fibre helps to prevent bad

cholesterol from being absorbed by the bloodstream instead of carrying it out of the body. A diet rich in oats can have a significant benefit and after just 6–8 weeks, blood pressure and cholesterol may be lowered in some patients.

CLEVER QUINOA

Quinoa is well known as an alternative to couscous but you can also buy it as flakes too. Use in healthy snacks in just the same way as porridge oats. Quinoa is rich in protein, containing all the essential amino acids or the building blocks of protein, and is one of only a very few plant sources to do this. It makes a great booster to any muesli bar or power ball mixed half and half with oats or in place of oats.

BUCKWHEAT

Not part of the wheat or grain family, the tiny triangular seeds come from a plant related to rhubarb. First grown some 4,000 years BC in the Balkans, Asia and the Middle East, buckwheat is rich in soluble fibre and contains magnesium which helps to relax the blood vessels, and to improve blood flow and nutrient delivery while lowering blood pressure. It also contains smaller amounts of manganese, copper and phosphorous and the flavonoid 'rutin' which aids the action of vitamin C and works as an antioxidant. Commonly available in the form of flakes.

RYE

Rye flakes are a robust cereal grain. They are dark in colour and have a deeper flavour compared to that of wheat and oats. Rye is a good source of dietary fibre and manganese, and may help to prevent gallstones and reduce the risk of type 2 diabetes. It is also very low in saturated fat, cholesterol and sodium. It is thought to help with weight loss efforts, help prevent various types of cancer, and even lower the chances of developing childhood asthma. Rye flakes can usually be used in any recipe that requires oats.

Above: Quinoa flakes.

Below: Buckwheat flakes.

Superfoods

A superfood is defined as "a nutrient-rich food considered to be especially beneficial for health and well-being". The ingredients we generally consider to be superfoods are those packed with high levels of antioxidants, polyphenols, vitamins and minerals.

A few are described here, there are many others. For health it's important to increase the range of nutritious foods in our diets rather than just focusing on a handful of foods that claim to be 'super', so the advice is to incorporate these nutrient-rich ingredients into a varied, balanced diet. And of course they feature in the energy balls, bars and snacks that follow!

APPLES
Naturally rich in energy-boosting fruit sugars, apples also contain pectin, the gum-like substance which sets jam. This helps to carry bad cholesterol from the body and may also help activate beneficial bacteria in the large intestine while adding vitamin C and boosting fibre.

BANANAS
This is the only fruit to contain tryptophan, which together with the vitamin B6 helps the body to produce serotonin, making it the natural good-mood food. Rich in fruit sugars and starch, bananas boost energy while the potassium they contain helps to regulate blood pressure.

BEETROOT
Beetroot or beet is a good source of iron and folate (naturally occurring folic acid), plus it also contains magnesium, betaine and other antioxidants. The juice of beetroot is used widely by athletes for its nitrates, as recent health claims suggest it can boost exercise performance. Other studies have also shown it can help to lower blood pressure, increase blood flow and prevent dementia. Adding naturally sweet beetroot means that you can reduce the amount of sugar needed.

BLUEBERRIES
These little berries are bursting with vitamin K, vitamin C, fibre, manganese and other antioxidants that fight off free radicals (molecules that cause cell damage and ageing), and may help protect against cancer and reduce the effects of age-related conditions. They contain a type of flavonoid known as anthocyanin, which give them their lovely colour (likewise with red cabbage, cranberries, and aubergines or eggplants). The fact that they can be eaten fresh and require no cooking is an added bonus!

CAULIFLOWER
This in-vogue vegetable belongs to the cruciferous family and contains sulforaphane, thought by some researchers to help slow the growth of some cancers, plus a range of vitamins, minerals, antioxidants and phytonutrients. It is also low in calories so is good news if you are watching your weight.

CHOCOLATE
Research into this delicious ingredient found that the Kuna Indians of Panama who drank cocoa as their main beverage had very low blood pressure, and further studies have shown that cocoa products, including dark or bittersweet chocolate, may help to slightly lower blood pressure. Cocoa is a good source of magnesium, manganese, phosphorous, iron and zinc, plus antioxidant catechins and procyanidins. But remember, it's the cocoa that contains all the good stuff – the darker your chocolate the better, milk chocolate doesn't count!

CRANBERRIES
Most well-known for helping to prevent urinary tract infections, cranberries are rich in antioxidants and may help protect against cancer and heart disease; they may even help prevent mouth ulcers and have anti-ageing properties.

GOJI BERRIES

Goji berries, also called the wolfberry, has been used in Chinese medicine for more than 6,000 years and they are alleged to boost the immune system and brain activity as well as protect against heart disease and cancer. They are rich in vitamin C, vitamin B2, vitamin A, selenium and iron.

KALE

Kale is very rich in fibre, as well as potassium, vitamin C and vitamin B6, and these nutrients are important in heart health. The fibre and water content promote a healthy digestive tract, whilst the high content of beta-carotene is essential for the growth of all bodily tissues, including skin and hair. Kale also contains an antioxidant known as alpha-lipoic acid which has been shown to lower glucose levels and increase insulin sensitivity.

MATCHA GREEN TEA

Sold in concentrated powdered form this green tea contains 137 times the amount of antioxidants than the same weight of regular green tea. Buy in small tea bags and soak in boiled water in the same way as making your usual herbal tea.

ORANGES

Sweet, juicy and aromatic, oranges are one of the most luscious citrus fruits. They are superfoods because they contain high concentrations of vitamin C, vitamin A, antioxidants, flavonoids, potassium, calcium, magnesium and dietary fibre. Oranges are one of the most popular snacks and they add a great taste to any recipe.

SEA SALAD
Seaweed offers an unparalleled range of vitamins, minerals and other beneficial nutrients. It contains anti-bacterial, anti-inflammatory and anti-viral properties. You can buy sea vegetables fresh and dried, and packets of mixed red, green and brown sea salad (often mixes of wakame, sugar kelp, nori and sea lettuce) are available in wholefood stores.

RAW CACAO
This is made by cold pressing unroasted cocoa beans, so removing the fat but retaining important antioxidants, minerals and the amino acid tryptophan which aids relaxation and sleep. The cocoa powder usually used in baking is darker in colour as it has been roasted at high temperatures, so lowering the overall nutritional value and giving it a stronger, slightly bitter taste.

SPIRULINA
A blue-green powder made from algae, spirulina contains 60% protein and useful amounts of vitamin B12, making it a great nutrient-booster for those following a vegan diet. It contains essential fatty acids and is also thought to have immune-boosting properties and may help normalize blood pressure.

TOMATOES
Tomatoes contain lycopene, an antioxidant rarely found in other foods, and studies have suggested that it could protect against certain cancers. The amount of lycopene available increases by 50% when the tomatoes are cooked. They are also rich in potassium, fibre and vitamin C.

WHEATGRASS
Wheatgrass contains chlorophyll, vitamin A, vitamin C, vitamin E, calcium, iron and magnesium, and is said to help with cleansing the blood and gastrointestinal tract.

Diet adaptations

Above: Porridge (rolled) oats, barley flakes, rye flakes and sesame seeds should be stored in airtight containers.

Opposite, top: There is no need to feel you are missing out with these delicious gluten- and dairy-free clementine & almond squares p128.

Opposite, bottom right: It is easy to boost protein on a vegan diet by adding spoonfuls of soya powder or soya milk in place of dairy milk.

GLUTEN-FREE

If you suffer with coeliac disease you will have to avoid gluten for life. Reducing gluten in your diet may also be useful if you suffer with digestive issues, such as bloating or flatulence, but otherwise do get some advice before cutting out a food group, as there may be other reasons why your digestion is playing up.

When cutting out foods, it's always good to focus on those you can have, rather than those you can't! There are lots of naturally gluten-free foods available – fruit, vegetables, eggs, fish, seafood, meat, poultry, dairy products, beans, legumes and nuts. And there are many naturally gluten-free grains that can be enjoyed – corn, teff, flax, chia, nut flours, amaranth, buckwheat, millet, quinoa, tapioca and rice.

Many recipes in the book are made with oats, which contain avenins rather than gluten. These can be tolerated by some people on a coeliac diet but not all, depending on their sensitivity, so always check with your health consultant before introducing into your diet. During harvesting, processing and storage, oats may be contaminated with wheat or even grown in adjacent fields to wheat. To make sure, always read the packaging to check that they are gluten-free before using, or swap the oats for the same weight of gluten-free buckwheat flakes instead.

You really don't need to miss out on great-tasting, energy-giving foods, especially with some of the simple recipes in this book that have no gluten in them, such as minted matcha & almond power balls p76, apricot & coconut power balls p86, or super-seedy buckwheat bars p110.

DAIRY-FREE

If you are aiming to avoid dairy due to an intolerance to lactose, there are now lots of other options available. But it is still important to find out which foods do contain dairy that you may not suspect at first, so read labels on the foods you buy just to make sure.

You can now buy lots of dairy milk alternatives, such as almond, soya, hemp, coconut etc., or you can make your own nut milks, and then use the leftover nuts for other recipes in the book. And if you are concerned about not getting enough calcium in your diet through lack of dairy, there are plenty of other calcium-rich foods you can include on a daily basis.

For dairy-free energy snacks you might like to try espresso supremo power balls p70, chocolate brownie balls p82, blueberry & chia balls p94, or clementine & almond squares p128.

VEGAN

Vegans obviously avoid many of the unhealthy substances found in animal products such as cholesterol and saturated fat, and they are likely to consume more vitamins, minerals and fibre due to eating lots of fruit and vegetables, but it's still important to ensure all the necessary nutrients are being consumed for a healthy lifestyle.

Getting enough protein is reliant on eating a large variety of plant proteins. Amino acids are the building blocks of protein and some of these cannot be made by your body, they only come from food. Animal proteins provide these in abundance, but vegans need to eat lots of nuts, legumes, tofu, pulses, grains and seeds to be sure they are consuming enough.

Other nutrients the vegan must be aware of are: calcium – needed for bone health (green leafy vegetables, seeds, pulses and grains); vitamin D – which is needed for the absorption of calcium (fortified products such as cereals, rice milk and soya milk); vitamin B12 – helps with red blood cell production (fortified cereals, soya milk and other products); zinc – (nuts, beans and soya products); and omega-3 fatty acids – important for heart health and brain function (oils and fortified foods).

PALEO

The paleo diet is built on the concept that the best diet is the one to which we are genetically adapted, with the premise that human genetics have hardly changed since the dawn of agriculture. Research has shown that the aged populations of hunter-gatherer societies were virtually free of high cholesterol, hypertension and other chronic diseases that have become endemic in Western societies.

There are a number of reasons why the paleo diet may be a healthy choice. Looking at it as a whole, and considering the body is made up of protein, carbohydrates, fats, water and oxygen, it makes sense that if you feed your body those nutrients in the cleanest form possible, then it will perform better. By eliminating processed foods you are automatically eating a low sugar and sodium diet (as long as you don't add salt to your cooking!), whilst increasing your intake of other great nutrients that come from fresh foods.

If you are starting this as a healthy-eating plan, start to make small changes that are sustainable – gradually change

Below, left to right: Indian-spiced mixed nuts, cauliflower munchies, and minted matcha & almond balls.

your diet to suit you and make sure the changes you make can be maintained for months or years, not just a few weeks.

Foods that can be eaten on the paleo diet are grass-produced meats, fish (wild if possible), seafood, fresh fruit (limit the amount if you are trying to reduce sugar in the diet as it is high in natural sugar), fresh vegetables, eggs (look for omega-3 enriched), nuts, seeds, and health oils such as olive, flaxseed, avocado, coconut, walnut.

All of these recipes can be eaten on the paleo diet: Indian-spiced mixed nuts p40, cauliflower munchies, without the dip p48, or minted matcha & almond balls p76.

FOR CHILDREN

Most children at some time or other decide that vegetables are to be avoided at all costs! But it's important to remember that you are responsible for helping them to eat as healthily as possible – so try to lead by example. Get them involved in making their own energy balls and muesli bars, adding ingredients they like (but keeping a watchful eye on the amount of sugary things that may go in). Some schools have a no-nut policy so check before adding these nutrient-dense snacks to a child's lunchbox. Power balls are more suitable for kids aged 7 and above. All of these recipes are perfect snacks for children to take to school – roasted kale crisps p44, cacao crispy bars p50, triple decker with apricot p104, or mini blueberry & orange loaves p130.

Top right: Quick and easy to prepare, kale crisps can be oven-roasted in just 7–10 minutes.

Eating for energy around exercise

Knowing when best to eat around training or doing exercise can really make a difference to your performance, especially if you are lacking in energy. It is important to figure out which foods or drinks work for you when you are training; never try anything new when you are taking part in a race for example, as you may suffer the consequences! There are different phases to consider when taking exercise: energy phase – just before and during exercise; anabolic phase (for example the growth of bone and increases in muscle mass) – the 45-minute window following a training session; and growth phase – the end of the anabolic phase to the start of the next session.

EATING FOR THE ENERGY PHASE
The key to efficient glycogen refuelling is to maintain steady levels of blood glucose and insulin, so controlling your blood-sugar balance by eating little and often. Eat 200–300g/ 7–11oz of carbohydrate 3–4 hours before exercise, to maximize your glycogen stores – make sure the meal is low in fat and fibre and high in fluids (the body takes longer to digest fat and fibre, but you need energy quickly). Good snack foods to eat just before training include bananas, oats and white bread. You might like to try cacao crispy bars p50 or espresso supremo power balls p70. Consuming carbohydrates during exercise is only necessary if training hard for longer than 60 minutes – most of the energy will come from glycogen stores in the liver and muscles. This also needs to be easily digested and absorbed. It's purely personal choice as to whether this is a drink or solids, but if it's solids, then liquid must also be consumed.

EATING FOR THE ANABOLIC PHASE
The anabolic phase is the 45-minute window after training, and this is when your muscles are ready to absorb the nutrients you have used up the most – storage is faster during post-exercise than at any other time. This is when most

athletes fail as they feel they have done their training and their mind moves on to something else. Eating carbohydrate with protein has also been shown to be more effective than just carbohydrate alone. Failure to replenish all the nutrients you have used – carbohydrates, proteins and fluids – during or after a workout can have a detrimental effect on the muscles and may decrease performance in the days that follow. You might like to try nutty trail mix p58, dark chocolate super-booster p64 or mixed seed power balls p81.

EATING FOR THE GROWTH PHASE

Protein has now been shown to be important throughout the day – it's not necessary to eat in the 45-minute window post exercise, but it is important to make sure you are eating enough throughout the day to replace what is being used through training, to ensure your muscles are rebuilt and repaired. During the growth stage it is important to maintain insulin sensitivity in order to continue to replenish glycogen stores and to maintain the anabolic state. Therefore consuming a carbohydrate- and protein-rich meal within 2 hours of exercise may have a positive effect, as well as maintaining good blood sugar balance and sufficient protein intake throughout the day. You might like to try summer berry & minted yogurt balls p90 or choc-dipped quinoa bars p106.

HYDRATION

Our bodies depend on water to survive – every cell, tissue and organ in the body needs water to function correctly. For example, the body uses water to maintain its temperature, transport nutrients to the cells, remove waste and lubricate joints. Rather than buying expensive isotonic sports drinks you can easily make your own by mixing together squash, water and a pinch of salt.

Exercise or rises in temperature increase perspiration, loss of water and hence fluid requirements.

Opposite, top to bottom: Oatylicious blueberry & vanilla bars p120, gingered beet & blackberry balls p78, and banana & cranberry muesli bars p102.

Below: There are a wide variety of travel cups available for carrying water and homemade isotonic drinks so you can stay hydrated throughout your day and during exercise.

Getting organised

A lot of people struggle with trying to eat a healthy diet whilst also leading a busy life, trying to incorporate work, family, hobbies and a social life! But as with anything, if you plan ahead it can all be made much easier. Include some of these energy-giving recipes into your daily diet and you will have made the first steps to improving your energy levels, enabling you to do more.

Keeping a 'Food & Mood' diary when you first start to change things in your diet is sometimes useful – you can gauge the changes your body is making, and find out what works for you and what doesn't.

Knowing which nutrients are required is only part of the picture. Now you need to fit them into your daily diet, here are a few rules to help you on your way –

- Always eat breakfast, aiming to include protein to help control blood sugar.
- Eat 3 meals and 2 snacks a day, also including protein in each one.
- Aim for at least 5 servings of fruit and vegetables a day – colourful fruit and vegetables ensure you are likely to be getting a good variety of vitamins and minerals.
- Cook everything from scratch – know what is going into your body, buy the freshest, cleanest food you can and cook it simply. Steam, boil or steam-fry foods rather than cooking at high temperatures. Raw food is also great but not all the time as some foods are hard to digest – lightly steaming is best.

THE BEST TIP OF ALL

Get organised – plan your diet! Do a big shop and cook lots of great dishes that you can tuck into over the next few days rather than leaving it all to the last minute when you will be tempted to grab the nearest unhealthy pre-packed food. Lots of the recipes in this book are perfect for making in advance and either freezing in small containers, or storing in plastic containers in the refrigerator, so you can just grab and go.

FREEZING KNOW-HOW

The recipes from the traybake bites chapter all freeze well. Cut into slices or pieces and wrap individually or in small packs either in clear film, plastic wrap or baking parchment and then pack into a plastic container. Label and seal tight with a lid. Use within 2 months.

Reduced-sugar muesli bars tend to go a little softer than those made with more traditional amounts of sugar and butter. Freezing is ideal and means that you can make up a batch at the weekend and then freeze in individually wrapped portions either in baking parchment or clear film and then packed into a plastic container. Label and use within 2 months.

Most power balls can also be frozen with the exception of those made with frozen fruits. Freeze in a single layer on a baking sheet until hard then transfer to a plastic container, interleaving the layers with non-stick baking parchment. Label and use within 1 month.

To defrost the items, pack into a lunchbox and leave at room temperature; they will defrost in 3–4 hours, just in time for lunch or an afternoon school or work snack.

BASIC EQUIPMENT

Chances are you will have most of the things needed for the recipes: measuring spoons, scales or American cup measures, baking parchment for lining tins or pans plus a 20cm/8in shallow square tin, and an 18 x 28 x 4cm/7 x 11 x 1½in rectangular traybake tin. If you don't have a rectangular cake tin you may have a small roasting pan the same size. A food processor blends the power balls together in just a couple of minutes. However if you don't have one, then finely chop all the ingredients with a large knife and then beat together in a bowl with nut milk or fruit juice. Once you have tried and enjoyed a few of the recipes then you may feel that this is a piece of equipment that would be worth the investment. A food processor also makes light work of blending cakes, smoothies or soups and will finely slice vegetables for salads.

Above: Mini blueberry & orange loaves can be stored in a plastic bag or container in the refrigerator for 3 days or you can freeze a batch to use within 2 months.

How to make power balls

Be right on trend with these nutrient-dense mini mouthfuls. Forget about munching on a bag of crisps or chocolate bar, these super-powered snacks are great to add to your bag and snack on after a gym workout or after a school activity, to boost protein and energy levels and fight fatigue. Made in a matter of minutes in the food processor then rolled into balls in the palm of your hands, these tasty snacks come in a wide range of flavours, colours and textures. Once you have tried a selection in this book try out your own flavour combos.

WHAT INGREDIENTS DO YOU NEED?
- Wholegrains, porridge (rolled) oats, buckwheat or quinoa flakes or your favourite choice of grain.
- Unblanched almonds or cashew nut pieces are the most popular nuts because of their mild creamy taste; add brazil nuts sparingly as they have a much stronger flavour, or try hazelnuts, pistachio or macadamia nuts.
- Nut butter or healthy olive, hemp or rapeseed oil to moisten and enrich the power balls.
- A small amount of liquid, unsweetened soya milk or nut milk, freshly squeezed orange juice or a small splash of water, if needed, to help bind the mixture together.
- An optional protein booster in the form of powdered whey, soya, hemp or pea protein, or a teaspoonful of spirulina, wheatgrass, baobab or moringa powder.

1 Add the chosen dry ingredients – nuts, seeds and grains – to the food processor bowl and blitz together until finely chopped.

2 Add the fruits, vegetables and any extra powders or flavourings and blitz again until the mixture begins to clump, adding a little liquid, if required.

3 Squeeze the mixture into a ball, take out of the processor bowl and cut into pieces. Roll each piece into a ball then pack into a plastic container, interleaving with layers of parchment.

Mix and match flavours to suit you
- A little cacao powder for a chocolately fix that is richer in antioxidants than more traditionally processed cocoa powder.
- Mix in a little chopped fresh mint, parsley or coriander (cilantro) for fresh breath confidence.

How to make muesli bars

Muesli bars or flapjacks have long been popular with all ages. The traditional versions are made with oats mixed with generous amounts of butter, sugar and syrup, and are full of energy but not very healthy. This book gives more modern takes on these favourite snacks, using less fat with reduced amounts of sugar, and additional flavour and nutrition provided by spices, dried fruit, fresh fruit, nuts and seeds.

WHAT INGREDIENTS DO YOU NEED?
• Fresh fruits, especially those classed as superfoods such as blueberries or bananas, make an excellent nutritional addition to any bar or flapjack.
• Grains are the basis of all muesli bars; choose from porridge (rolled) oats, buckwheat, rye or quinoa flakes.
• Adding seeds and nuts is an easy way to boost protein levels. As they do not contain the whole range of amino acids that the body needs to make protein, combine with other foods such as soya products and grains.

1 Preheat the oven to the temperature required by the recipe, usually 180°C/350°F/Gas 4 for most muesli bars.

2 Gently heat the fats and sugars, or sugar alternatives, in a pan until they have all melted and dissolved.

3 Stir in the dry ingredients, such as grains and flours. Mix in any seeds, dried or fresh fruits and nuts required in the recipe until all combined.

4 Tip the mixture into a baking parchment-lined tin or pan, press flat then bake until golden; depending on the recipe this usually takes between 15–30 minutes.

5 Cut into bars while hot, then leave to cool and harden. Remove from the tin and store in a plastic container in the refrigerator.

Mix and match flavours to suit you
• Add a little ground cinnamon, ginger or mixed (apple pie) spice.
• Try a little finely grated lemon, lime or orange zest or a mix of the three for a zingy freshness.

CLUSTERS AND QUICK FIXES

There are just some moments when you need to grab a quick snack. Don't worry if you haven't been shopping, chances are you will have most of the ingredients in the cupboard already. These healthy snacks can be mixed together in literally a matter of minutes.

Spice-crusted chickpea nibbles

Chickpeas are great in more things than hummus. Try them as a super-speedy spiced alternative to crisps. Low in fat, they make a good protein-rich snack, and as chickpeas contain complex carbs they take longer for the body to break down, giving a slow-release energy boost.

Gluten-free
Dairy-free
Vegan

Serves 4
Prep: 5 mins, including cooking

400g/14oz can chickpeas in water
4 tsp/20ml olive oil
1 tsp/5ml cumin seeds, roughly crushed
½ tsp/2.5ml fennel seeds, roughly crushed
1 tbsp/15ml sesame seeds
1 tsp/5ml mild smoked paprika
1 tbsp/15ml ground linseeds
2 tsp/10ml maple syrup
Pinch salt

1 Drain the chickpeas into a colander, rinse with cold water, drain again then dry with kitchen paper.

2 Warm the oil in a large frying pan then add the cumin, fennel and sesame seeds and cook over a medium heat for 1 minute to release the flavour, then take off the heat and stir in the paprika.

3 Tip the chickpeas into the frying pan, sprinkle with the ground linseeds and stir well to coat in the spice mix. Cook over a medium to high heat, stirring until the spice forms a dry crust. Drizzle with the maple syrup, sprinkle with a little salt and cook briefly until the syrup has caramelised.

4 Leave to cool then eat while just warm served in baking parchment cones, or cool completely and pack into small jars or plastic containers. Store in the refrigerator for up to 2 days.

COOK'S TIP If you like chilli or foods with a bit of heat then add ¼ tsp/1.5ml of hot smoked paprika instead of the mild or sweet version. The hot smoked paprika has the same kind of heat as chilli powder but with the addition of a lovely smoky barbecue flavour.

Energy 139kcal/581kJ; Protein 6.6g; Carbohydrate 12.8g, of which sugars 1.8g; Fat 7.6g, of which saturates 1.1g; Cholesterol 0mg; Calcium 75mg; Fibre 4.2g; Sodium 148mg.

Indian-spiced mixed nuts

Gluten-free
Dairy-free
Vegan
No added sugar

Serves 4
Prep: 5 mins, including
cooking

1 tbsp/15ml olive oil
50g/2oz/ ⅓ cup cashew nuts
50g/2oz/ ⅓ cup unblanched
almonds
50g/2oz/⅓ cup small brazil
nuts
50g/2oz/generous ⅓ cup
pecan nuts
1 tsp/5ml turmeric
1 tsp/5ml ground garam
masala
¼ tsp/1.5ml dried chilli,
crushed (optional)
Pinch salt

Rather than reach for a pack of highly-salted and processed crisps, choose protein-packed nuts that are flavoured with aromatic spices for a tasty and quick-to-make snack.

1 Heat the oil in a frying pan, add the nuts and fry over a medium heat for 1–2 minutes, stirring until lightly toasted. Add the spices, crushed chilli if using, and salt, and fry, stirring for 1 minute until the nuts are well coated in the spice mix and just beginning to darken.

2 Leave to cool then eat while still warm or cool completely then pack into individual jars or plastic containers. Screw or clip on the lids. Store in a cool place for up to 3 days.

NUTRITION TIP Turmeric has long been popular in South Asian cooking and is regarded in Ayurvedic medicine as a complementary treatment for pain, inflammation, infection and gastrointestinal problems. Turmeric may also help with arthritis.

COOK'S TIP Mix and match the nuts depending on the types that you have, aiming for a total of 200g/7oz/1⅓ cups. If you don't have quite enough then make up the weight with pumpkin seeds and/or sunflower seeds.

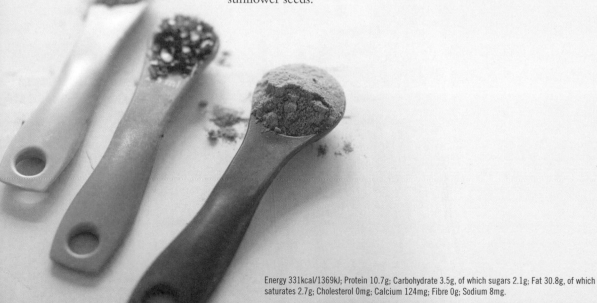

Energy 331kcal/1369kJ; Protein 10.7g; Carbohydrate 3.5g, of which sugars 2.1g; Fat 30.8g, of which saturates 2.7g; Cholesterol 0mg; Calcium 124mg; Fibre 0g; Sodium 8mg.

Oriental-spiced edamame beans

Getting the kids to eat vegetables can be tricky, but offering them as a small snack rather than part of a main meal might just be all it takes.

1 Bring a pan of water to the boil, add the frozen edamame beans and simmer for 3 minutes.

2 Meanwhile, dry fry the seeds in a non-stick frying pan for 2 minutes, stirring until lightly toasted and the sesame seeds are just beginning to jump about in the pan. Drizzle over the soy sauce and maple syrup and stir together, then take off the heat.

3 Drain the beans into a colander, rinse with cold water to cool quickly then drain again. Layer the edamame beans and seed mixture into small paper cups lined with baking parchment and serve immediately. Or if eating later pack into small plastic containers or jars and screw or clip on the lids, however they are best eaten on the day they are made.

NUTRITION TIP Frozen edamame beans, or baby soya beans, make a great standby food. Just like frozen peas they are rich in fibre, but unlike frozen peas they are also rich in protein. We need protein for growth, repair and maintenance of cells in our bones, muscles, hair, even our nails, and to help create enzymes to aid digestion and antibodies to fight off infection.

Gluten-free,
but check on brand of
soy sauce
Dairy-free
Vegan

Serves 4
Prep: 5 mins
Cook: 5 mins

350g/12oz/2¼ cups frozen
edamame beans
2 tbsp/30ml sesame seeds
2 tbsp/30ml sunflower seeds
2 tbsp/30ml pumpkin seeds
4 tsp/20ml reduced-salt soy
sauce
2 tsp/10ml maple syrup

Energy 265kcal/1103kJ; Protein 17.1g; Carbohydrate 9.1g, of which sugars 3.8g; Fat 18g,
of which saturates 2.6g; Cholesterol 0mg; Calcium 137mg; Fibre 9.1g; Sodium 182mg.

Roasted kale crisps

Gluten-free,
but check on brand of
soy sauce
Dairy-free
Vegan

Serves 4
Prep: 5 mins
Cook: 7–10 mins

175g/6oz/6 large handfuls
kale leaves, washed, drained
well and thickly sliced
2 tbsp/30ml olive oil
2 tbsp/30ml reduced-salt soy
sauce
2 tsp/10ml molasses sugar or
syrup
2.5cm/1in piece fresh root
ginger, peeled, coarsely
grated

Kale has become the favourite healthy option and is available in all supermarkets and farmers' markets, plus it is easy to grow even for those new to gardening.

1 Preheat the oven to 150°C/300°F/Gas 2. Dry the kale well with kitchen paper then add to a large bowl. Drizzle the oil, soy sauce and molasses over then add the ginger. Toss together to mix well and flavour all the leaves.

2 Divide the flavoured kale mixture between two large baking sheets and spread into a thin layer.

3 Bake for 4–5 minutes until the kale leaves around the edges of the baking sheet are beginning to crisp up. Move the kale from the outer edges into the centre and those in the centre to the edges and cook for 3–5 minutes more until all the kale pieces are crisp and dry.

4 Leave to cool for 15 minutes then enjoy while still warm and crisp or leave to cool completely and pack into a lidded plastic container, to store in the refrigerator. However the kale is best eaten on the day of making.

NUTRITION TIP Kale is rich in lutein and zeaxanthin, two cancer-fighting antioxidants, plus vitamins C and K, chlorophyll and iron which assist with the oxygenation and health of red blood cells, and so help to fight fatigue. COOK'S TIP Try to buy whole kale leaves so that you can slice them thickly; some supermarkets sell bags of thickly sliced kale, if you can only get bags of thinly sliced kale then reduce the cooking time down to 3–4 minutes, stir and then cook for a further 3–4 minutes.

Energy 72kcal/299kJ; Protein 1.6g; Carbohydrate 2.6g, of which sugars 2.5g; Fat 6.2g, of which saturates 0.9g; Cholesterol 0mg; Calcium 71mg; Fibre 1.8g; Sodium 290mg.

Sun-dried tomato & Parmesan popcorn

Forget about sweet sugary popcorn, this cheesy version will soon convert you. Popcorn is a natural wholegrain and a good source of complex carbohydrates. On its own popcorn is super-healthy, it is the not-so-healthy fast food synthetic-tasting flavours that are not.

1 Add the oil and rosemary to a medium pan, warm together for a minute or two to release the rosemary flavour then spoon out 3 tbsp/45ml oil into a bowl and mix with the paprika and tomato paste.

2 Add the popping corn to the pan, cover with a lid and cook over a medium heat for 3–4 minutes until the popcorn has all popped, shaking the pan from time to time.

3 Remove the lid, drizzle over the tomato mixture, add the Parmesan and toss together. Serve warm or cold.

YOU MIGHT ALSO LIKE TO TRY.....
• Chilli popcorn: instead of the rosemary, infuse the olive oil with ½–1 red chilli, thickly sliced with the seeds left in for fans of super-hot foods, or take out the seeds for a milder chilli taste. Add the paprika and tomato oil but leave out the Parmesan.
• Balsamic popcorn: simply drizzle the rosemary-flavoured or plain popcorn with a little balsamic vinegar.

Gluten-free
No added sugar

Serves 4–6
Prep: 5 mins
Cook: 5 mins

4 tbsp/60ml olive oil
2 rosemary stems, torn into pieces
½ tsp/2.5ml mild paprika
2 tsp/10ml sun-dried tomato paste
200g/7oz/1 cup popping corn
30g/1oz piece Parmesan cheese, finely grated

Energy 218kcal/909kJ; Protein 3.9g; Carbohydrate 16.3g, of which sugars 0.4g; Fat 15.8g, of which saturates 2.4g; Cholesterol 5mg; Calcium 55mg; Fibre 0g; Sodium 39mg.

Cauliflower munchies

These crispy cauliflower bites make a great alternative to carb- and fat-loaded chips, and taste just as good hot or cold. If you don't serve them with the dip, they are vegan and dairy-free too.

1 Heat the oil in a large non-stick frying pan, add the spice mix and garlic and heat over a low heat for 1 minute to release the flavour of the spice mix.

2 Add the cauliflower and increase the heat to medium, then stir-fry for 3–4 minutes until the cauliflower is just beginning to brown around the edges and is hot but still crisp.

3 Sprinkle with the paprika and a little salt and serve on their own or with the yogurt flavoured with the chopped mint, if liked.

NUTRITION TIP Cauliflower has been found to contain sulphurous compounds which may help to protect us from cancer, plus it contains immune-boosting vitamin C.
COOK'S TIP Za'atar spice mix is made up of sesame seeds, dried thyme, oregano, sumac and cumin seeds and is now available in larger supermarkets or ethnic grocers. It is popular all over the Middle East and is often sprinkled over flatbreads before baking.

Gluten-free
No added sugar

Serves 4
Prep: 10 mins, including
cooking

2 tbsp/30ml olive oil
1 tbsp/15ml za'atar spice mix
2 garlic cloves, thinly sliced
1 cauliflower, cut into florets,
core and leaves discarded
1 tsp/5ml mild paprika
A little coarse salt

To serve (optional)
200g/7oz/¾ cup 0%-fat Greek
(US strained plain) yogurt
3 tbsp/45ml fresh chopped
mint

Energy 96kcal/396kJ; Protein 4.7g; Carbohydrate 4.2g, of which sugars 3.1g; Fat 6.8g, of which saturates 1.1g; Cholesterol 0mg; Calcium 29mg; Fibre 3g; Sodium 12mg.

Cacao crispy bars

Gluten-free
Dairy-free
Vegan

Cuts into 12
Prep: 15 mins
Chill: 15 minutes

3 tbsp/45ml smooth almond
or cashew nut butter
3 tbsp/45ml maple syrup
3 tbsp/45ml coconut oil
2 tbsp/30ml light olive oil
3 tbsp/45ml cacao powder
1 tsp/5ml vanilla extract
50g/2oz/1½ cups plain puffed
rice

NUTRITION TIP This recipe
uses plain puffed rice found
in health food stores or
larger supermarkets; don't
get it confused with the
breakfast cereals coated
with refined sugar.

For fans of old-fashioned chocolate crispy cakes made
with breakfast cereal this modern version is made with
almond butter, coconut oil, cacao powder and maple
syrup. Super-easy to do and the perfect beginners' recipe
for kids to make.

1 Cut a piece of baking parchment a little larger than a
20cm/8in shallow square baking tin or pan, snip diagonally
into the corners then press the paper into the tin so that base
and sides are lined.

2 Add the nut butter, maple syrup and coconut oil to a pan
and warm over a low heat, stirring until melted and smooth.
Take off the heat and mix in the olive oil, cacao powder and
vanilla until smooth, then stir in the puffed rice.

3 Tip the mixture into the lined tin, press into an even layer
then chill for 15 minutes or longer if you have time.

4 Lift out of the tin holding the paper. Cut into 12 pieces, lift
off the paper and pack into a plastic box. Eat within 2 days.

Energy 106kcal/439kJ; Protein 1.1g; Carbohydrate 6.9g, of which sugars 2.4g; Fat 8.5g, of which saturates 4.2g; Cholesterol 0mg; Calcium 3mg; Fibre 0.2g; Sodium 0mg.

Apple & pecan clusters

Gluten-free
Dairy-free

Makes 12
Prep: 10 mins
Cook: 12–15 mins

2 tbsp/30ml olive oil

2 tbsp/30ml soya margarine

2 tbsp/30ml light muscovado (brown) sugar

2 tbsp/30ml clear honey

50g/2oz/½ cup buckwheat flakes

25g/1oz/¼ cup quinoa flakes

50g/2oz/generous ⅓ cup pecan nuts, halved

2 tbsp/30ml hulled hemp seeds

2 tbsp/30ml pumpkin seeds

1 small dessert apple, cored, coarsely grated

1 tsp/5ml ground cinnamon

1 egg white

Don't have time for breakfast or want something to nibble on after an early morning workout? Then pack a few of these crispy bites into a small plastic container ready to go.

1 Preheat the oven to 180°C/350°F/Gas 4. Lightly oil a 12-section mini muffin tin or pan, or separate 12 mini paper cases and put on to a baking sheet.

2 Warm the oil, margarine, sugar and honey together until the margarine and sugar have melted. Take the pan off the heat and stir in the flakes, pecan nuts, seeds, grated apple and cinnamon.

3 Whisk the egg white with a fork in a small bowl until frothy then stir into the buckwheat mix.

4 Spoon rough-shaped mounds into the 12 sections of the mini muffin tin or paper cases. Bake for about 12–15 minutes until golden brown. Leave to cool for 10 minutes then loosen the edges with a knife, take out of the tin, if using, and cool on a wire rack.

5 Pack into a plastic container, press or clip on the lid and store in the refrigerator for up to 3 days.

NUTRITION TIP Although buckwheat flakes sound as if they are a no-no on a gluten-free/wheat-free diet, they actually come from the seeds of a plant related to the rhubarb family and are fine if following a coeliac diet, but always double check with the packaging to make sure they have not been processed with wheat grains. Like buckwheat we all think of quinoa as a grain but again this is actually a seed and is gluten-free.

Energy 123kcal/513kJ; Protein 1.9g; Carbohydrate 10.2g, of which sugars 6.2g; Fat 8.6g, of which saturates 1.6g; Cholesterol 7mg; Calcium 7mg; Fibre 2.2g; Sodium 87mg.

Cacao, cranberry & almond clusters

A sweet chocolately fix but made with just a small amount of muscovado sugar and healthier cacao, plus seeds, nuts and fibre-rich, wholegrain and cholesterol-lowering oats for a high-energy and moreish snack.

1 Preheat the oven to 180°C/350°F/Gas 4. Lightly oil a large roasting pan.

2 Warm the oil, margarine, sugar and cinnamon together in a pan, stirring until the margarine and sugar have melted.

3 Take the pan off the heat and stir in the seeds, almonds and oats and mix well. Lightly whisk the egg white in a small bowl with a fork until frothy then stir into the oat mixture.

4 Spread into an even layer in the roasting pan and cook for 8–10 minutes, stir so that the browner mixture from the edges are moved to the centre. Cook for 5 more minutes until all the mixture is evenly browned.

5 Sprinkle with the cranberries and cacao and leave to cool and crisp up in the pan.

6 Break the mixture into bitesize pieces and transfer to a plastic container and store in the refrigerator for up to 3 days.

NUTRITION TIP Cacao has been growing in popularity and is now sold in supermarkets and not just health food stores. Unlike standard cocoa powder it is made by cold-pressing unroasted cocoa beans so removing the fat and keeping the important antioxidants, minerals and the amino acid tryptophan which aids relaxation and sleep. COOK'S TIP If you only have standard cocoa in the cupboard then use this but stir into the just-melted sugar mixture before adding the oats and baking, so that it doesn't taste bitter.

Dairy-free

Serves 4
Prep: 10 mins
Cook: 13–15 mins

2 tbsp/30ml olive oil

2 tbsp/30ml soya margarine

2 tbsp/30ml light muscovado (brown) sugar

1 tsp/5ml ground cinnamon

2 tbsp/30ml hulled hemp seeds

2 tbsp/30ml sunflower seeds

50g/2oz/⅓ cup unblanched almonds, roughly chopped

50g/2oz/½ cup porridge (rolled) oats

1 egg white

3 tbsp/45ml dried cranberries

1 tbsp/15ml cacao powder

Energy 387kcal/1613kJ; Protein 9.1g; Carbohydrate 30.3g, of which sugars 16.5g; Fat 26.3g, of which saturates 5.1g; Cholesterol 21mg; Calcium 60mg; Fibre 5.7g; Sodium 153mg.

Superfood chocolate buttons

Forget about sugary-sweet chocolate buttons sold to kids, these giant-sized chocolate buttons are super-dark and moreish, and fab for grown-ups. Top with two different combos of protein-rich nuts and energy-boosting dried fruits.

1 Line 2 baking sheets with baking parchment. Melt the chocolate in a bowl set over a pan of gently simmering water. When softened stir briefly until smooth and glossy.

2 Drop teaspoonfuls of melted chocolate spaced well apart on to the lined sheets and spread with the back of a teaspoon to make circles about 4cm/1½in in diameter.

3 For the nutty-topped buttons, heat a dry frying pan, add the nuts and cook for a minute or two until lightly toasted. Drizzle the honey or maple syrup over and cook for 1–2 minutes more until caramelised. Spoon the nuts over half of the chocolate buttons and then sprinkle with the orange zest.

4 For the super-fruity topping sprinkle the dried fruits over the remaining chocolate buttons. Chill both sheets in the refrigerator for 10 minutes until set. Then transfer to a plastic container layered with baking parchment. Keep in the refrigerator for up to 3 days.

NUTRITION TIP The higher the cocoa solids in the dark chocolate the more phenylethylamine, which is the same chemical that your brain creates when you feel as if you are falling in love. No wonder we reach for the chocolate when we feel a little down.
COOK'S TIP Not all chocolate is suitable for those following a coeliac diet, so check the packaging before use.

Gluten-free,
if gluten-free chocolate
is used
Vegan,
if maple syrup is used

Makes 40
Prep: 15 mins
Chill: 10 mins

100g/3¾oz dark (bittersweet) chocolate, broken into pieces

Go nuts
2 tbsp/30ml pistachio nuts, roughly chopped
2 tbsp/30ml unblanched almonds, roughly chopped
4 brazil nuts, roughly chopped
1 tbsp/15ml honey or maple syrup
Zest of 1 medium orange, finely grated

Super-fruity
2 tsp/10ml dried goji berries
6 ready-to-eat dried apricots, roughly chopped
1 tbsp/15ml dried cranberries, roughly chopped

Energy 28kcal/117kJ; Protein 0.6g; Carbohydrate 2.8g, of which sugars 2.7g; Fat 1.7g, of which saturates 0.5g; Cholesterol 0mg; Calcium 7mg; Fibre 0.2g; Sodium 1mg.

Nutty trail mix

Have a small jar of this in your desk drawer or gym bag for a power-boosting, high-protein snack that keeps the hunger pangs at bay.

Gluten-free
Dairy-free
Vegan
No added sugar

Serves 4
Prep: 5 minutes

50g/2oz/⅓ cup small brazil nuts, halved

50g/2oz/⅓ cup cashew nuts

50g/2oz/generous ⅓ cup pecan nuts

2 tbsp/30ml pumpkin seeds

75g/3oz/⅓ cup ready-to-eat dried apricots, quartered

3 tbsp/45ml dried cranberries

3 tbsp/45ml dried goji berries

3 tbsp/45ml dried coconut flakes

1 Add all the ingredients to a bowl and stir together, then spoon into 4 individual jars or plastic containers.

2 Seal well with a screw or clip-on lid and keep in a cool dry place for up to 1 week.

NUTRITION TIP While nuts are rich in protein they are unfortunately quite high in calories at around 550 calories per 100g/3¾oz, which is due to the fat they contain. Luckily most nuts contain healthier unsaturated fat and these essential fatty acids are vital for normal tissue growth and development. Coconut oil is the exception as it contains saturated fat, with dried desiccated coconut containing slightly smaller amounts.

COOK'S TIP Pack the trail mix into portion-sized containers as it is all too easy to graze your way through a much larger amount than you had anticipated.

Energy 364kcal/1517kJ; Protein 11.1g; Carbohydrate 26.2g, of which sugars 24.1g; Fat 24.6g, of which saturates 2.2g; Cholesterol 0mg; Calcium 121mg; Fibre 2.7g; Sodium 14mg.

Apple & cinnamon thins

Many children won't tackle eating a whole apple, but by very thinly slicing and then slow cooking in the oven, these wafer-thin slices become more like sweet crisps. An easy, healthy snack to make.

Gluten-free
Dairy-free
Nut-free
No added sugar

Serves 6
Prep: 10 mins
Cook: 1¼–2 hours

2 tsp/10ml salt
3 dessert apples
A little ground cinnamon

1 Preheat the oven to 80°C/175°F/Gas – very low. If your oven does not have a setting this low then use 110°C/225°F/Gas ¼ but reduce the cooking time as this temperature tends to get the apples too brown. Stir the salt into a bowl of cold water then very thinly slice the apples and add to the bowl to stop them going brown.

2 Drain the apple slices and pat dry with kitchen paper. Arrange in a single layer on a large wire cooling rack set over a baking sheet.

3 Bake for 1¼–2 hours or until the slices are dry, Check on them after 45 minutes and move those slices that are browning around the edge of the wire rack to the centre and those in the centre to the outer edge so that they cook evenly.

4 Loosen the apple slices with a palette knife and leave on the cooling rack. Sprinkle with the cinnamon, then leave to cool completely.

5 Pack the slices into a small plastic container and seal well. Store in the refrigerator and eat within 2 days.

NUTRITION TIP Naturally rich in energy-boosting fruit sugars, apples also contain pectin, the gum–like substance which sets jam. This helps to carry bad cholesterol from the body and may also help activate beneficial bacteria in the large intestine.

Energy 24kcal/100kJ; Protein 0.2g; Carbohydrate 5.9g, of which sugars 5.9g; Fat 0.1g, of which saturates 0g; Cholesterol 0mg; Calcium 2mg; Fibre 1.2g; Sodium 2mg.

POWER BALLS

With gym memberships and fun runs gaining in popularity a high-protein and energy-boosting snack that can be made at home is a great way to enhance your performance pre- and post-workout. Make up a batch of power balls and store in the refrigerator, then you can just take out as many as you need, when you need them, add them to a smaller container and tuck into your sports bag for a portable healthy snack.

**Dairy-free
Vegan
No added sugar**

Makes 24
Prep: 10 mins

150g/5oz/8 Medjool dates,
stoned (pitted)
40g/1½oz/⅓ cup unflavoured
soya protein powder
150g/5oz/1½ cups porridge
(rolled) oats
50g/2oz/⅓ cup unblanched
almonds
110g/4oz/½ cup
unsweetened crunchy peanut
butter
100g/3¾oz/1 bar dark
(bittersweet) chocolate,
broken into pieces
4 tbsp/60ml unsweetened
almond milk
Pinch salt

Dark chocolate super-booster

Packed with protein these power balls will help build muscle mass, to aid your gym weight training, or boost energy if battling through a heavy work schedule.

1 Add the dates, protein powder, oats and almonds to a food processor and blitz together until finely chopped.

2 Add the peanut butter, chocolate, almond milk and salt and mix briefly until the chocolate and nuts are roughly chopped and still quite chunky and the mixture is beginning to clump together.

3 Squeeze the mixture into a ball, take out of the processor bowl and cut into 24 pieces. Roll each piece in the palm of your hands to make a smooth ball.

4 Pack into a plastic container, interleaving with layers of baking parchment. Store in the refrigerator for up to 3 days.

COOK'S TIP If you are not following a dairy-free or vegan diet you may prefer to use whey protein powder instead, choose the plain or vanilla-flavoured.

Energy 110kcal/462kJ; Protein 4.1g; Carbohydrate 12.3g, of which sugars 7.3g; Fat 5.3g, of which saturates 1.4g; Cholesterol 0mg; Calcium 14mg; Fibre 1.1g; Sodium 21mg.

Super-powered spirulina balls

Spirulina gives these protein-packed power balls their incredible colour, and while they may look as if they should be served at a Halloween party they are naturally sweet and moreish. If you make your own nut milk then use some of the soaked nuts in place of the dried ones.

1 Add the porridge oats and nuts to a food processor and blitz until finely chopped. Add the apricots and sunflower seeds and blitz again briefly until roughly chopped.

2 Spoon in the cashew butter, maple syrup, sea salad, if using, hemp and spirulina powder then add the orange juice. Blitz again until the mixture begins to clump together then add the milk and mix again briefly.

3 Squeeze the mixture together, take out of the processor bowl and cut into 20 pieces. Roll each piece in the palm of your hands to make a smooth ball. Press a goji berry into the top of each power ball.

4 Pack into a plastic container, interleaving with layers of baking parchment. Store in the refrigerator for up to 3 days.

NUTRITION TIP Spirulina is a blue–green powder made from algae and contains 60% protein and useful amounts of vitamin B12, making it a great nutrient-booster for those following a vegan diet. Hemp powder, like spirulina, is also a good protein-booster and contains omega-3 and -6 fatty acids and vitamin E. Buy as shelled seeds and oil too.

**Dairy-free
Vegan**

Makes 20
Prep: 10 mins

110g/4oz/1 cup porridge (rolled) oats

75g/3oz/½ cup cashew nut pieces

100g/3¾oz/½ cup ready-to-eat dried apricots

3 tbsp/45ml sunflower seeds

2 tbsp/30ml cashew nut butter

1 tbsp/15ml maple syrup

1 tbsp/15ml dried sea salad (optional)

2 tsp/10ml hemp powder

2 tsp/10ml spirulina powder

Juice of 1 orange

2–3 tbsp/30–45ml unsweetened almond milk

20 dried goji berries

Energy 86kcal/360kJ; Protein 2.5g; Carbohydrate 10g, of which sugars 4.5g; Fat 4.3g, of which saturates 0.7g; Cholesterol 0mg; Calcium 13mg; Fibre 1.5g; Sodium 7mg.

Double peanut energy balls

Vegan
Dairy-free
No added sugar

Makes 16
Prep: 10 mins

110g/4oz/5 Medjool dates, stoned (pitted)

110g/4oz/1 cup porridge (rolled) oats

2 tbsp/30ml ground flaxseeds

2 tbsp/30ml unsweetened crunchy peanut butter

75g/3oz/½ cup roasted salted peanuts

3 tbsp/45ml unsweetened almond milk

There are just some moments when you need a salty fix. These power balls are flecked with chunky pieces of roasted peanut and make a great protein- and energy-booster after a strenuous gym workout or long run. The added salt helps to replace the salts that you have lost through sweating, but do make sure to drink plenty of water to rehydrate too.

1 Add the dates and oats to a food processor and blitz until finely chopped.

2 Add the flaxseeds, peanut butter and peanuts then add the almond milk and blend briefly until the mixture begins to clump together and the nuts are still quite chunky.

3 Squeeze the mixture into a ball, take out of the processor and cut into 16 pieces. Roll each piece in the palm of your hands to make a smooth ball. Pack into a plastic container, interleaving with layers of baking parchment. Store in the refrigerator for up to 3 days.

NUTRITION TIP A jar of good peanut butter will contain 26.9g of protein per 100g which is pretty good. Choose a brand without added sugar, salt or palm oil. Peanuts are also a good source of B vitamins and minerals, copper, phosphorous, magnesium and zinc.

Energy 94kcal/394kJ; Protein 3.1g; Carbohydrate 11.2g, of which sugars 5.1g; Fat 4.4g, of which saturates 0.7g; Cholesterol 0mg; Calcium 10mg; Fibre 1.8g; Sodium 17mg.

Espresso supremo power balls

Naturally sweet Medjool dates, coconut, chia seeds and toasted hazelnuts mixed with strong espresso coffee make this a winning early morning gym combo.

1 Line the base of the grill or broiling pan with a piece of foil, fold up the edges then grill the hazelnuts for 2–3 minutes until lightly toasted. Rub in a kitchen towel to remove the brown skins.

2 Add the dates to a food processor with the oats and chia seeds, and blitz briefly until roughly chopped. Spoon in the hazelnuts, coconut, cacao and maple syrup, and then the coffee. Blitz together until finely chopped and beginning to clump together.

3 Squeeze the mixture into a ball, take out of the processor bowl and cut into 20 pieces. Roll each piece in the palm of your hands to a make smooth ball. Pack into a plastic container, interleaving with layers of baking parchment. Store in the refrigerator for up to 3 days.

NUTRITION TIP Mixing naturally sweet dates with protein-rich nuts and high-fibre oats will give the body a slow sustained energy boost rather than the rapid and subsequent low that you get when eating a bought chocolate bar.

Vegan
Dairy-free

Makes 20
Prep: 15 mins
Cook: 2–3 mins

50g/2oz/⅓ cup unblanched hazelnuts

150g/5oz/8 Medjool dates, stoned (pitted)

150g/5oz/1½ cups porridge (rolled) oats

2 tbsp/30ml chia seeds

40g/1½oz/½ cup unsweetened desiccated (dry shredded) coconut

1 tbsp/15ml cacao powder

1 tbsp/15ml maple syrup

4 tbsp/60ml or 1 espresso shot of black coffee

Energy 90kcal/377kJ; Protein 2.1g; Carbohydrate 11.5g, of which sugars 5.8g; Fat 4.2g, of which saturates 1.3g; Cholesterol 0mg; Calcium 20mg; Fibre 2.5g; Sodium 26mg.

Pistachio cheesecake bites

Calcium-rich

Makes 20
Prep: 15 mins

250g/9oz/1 cup reduced-fat
mascarpone
2 tsp/10ml maple syrup
2 tbsp/30ml ground flaxseeds
1 tsp/5ml chia seeds
1 tsp/5ml vanilla extract
25g/1oz/2 tbsp pistachio nuts
25g/1oz/2 tbsp pumpkin
seeds
1 tsp/5ml hemp or
wheatgrass powder (optional)

Tiny creamy bites that taste like cheesecake but are made in minutes, packed with healthy seeds and rolled in high-protein pale green pistachio nuts.

1 Add the mascarpone and maple syrup to a mixing bowl then stir in the flaxseeds, chia seeds and vanilla. Scoop out 20 teaspoonfuls of the mixture on to a large plate.

2 Finely chop the nuts and pumpkin seeds with a knife or food processor then put on to a second plate and mix with the hemp or wheatgrass powder, if using.

3 Roll the cheesy spoonfuls into the nut mix to make even-shaped balls then chill until firm. Pack into a plastic box interleaving with layers of baking parchment. Store in the refrigerator for up to 3 days.

NUTRITION TIP Health specialists used to say that fat was the baddie and advocated low-fat dairy or to avoid where possible, but it is now thought that too much sugar in the diet is more harmful. The key to eating a healthy diet is to eat a little from a wide range of foods.

Energy 50kcal/206kJ; Protein 2.1g;
Carbohydrate 1.6g, of which sugars 0.4g; Fat
3.9g, of which saturates 1.6g; Cholesterol 6mg;
Calcium 16mg; Fibre 0.9g; Sodium 57mg.

Good-for-you truffles

Traditional chocolate truffles are made with cream and booze; this easy child-friendly version is made with low-fat French-style soft goat's cheese, antioxidant-boosting cacao, protein powder and energy-boosting dates sneaked in for natural sweetness and flavour.

1 Melt the chocolate in a shallow dish set over a pan of gently simmering water.

2 Add the dates to a food processor and blitz until a smooth paste forms. Add the goat's cheese, coconut, cacao and protein powder then spoon in the maple syrup, vanilla and cinnamon. Blitz briefly together then add the melted chocolate and blitz until just mixed.

3 Scoop out rough-shaped teaspoonfuls of the chocolate mixture on to a baking sheet lined with baking parchment until you have 20 even-sized mounds. Chill for 30 minutes to firm up.

4 Smooth each chilled ball by rolling one at a time in your hand then roll one third of the balls in the coconut, one third in the grated chocolate and the rest in the cranberries until evenly coated.

5 Pack into a plastic container interleaving the layers with baking parchment. Chill in the refrigerator up to 3 days.

NUTRITION TIP Goat's milk is richer than cow's milk in vitamins A, B, D and K and a range of minerals such as calcium, iron, phosphorous, magnesium and potassium. It also has less lactose and a smaller fat structure, so making soft goat's cheese easier to digest for some people who have trouble with cow's milk cheeses.

Gluten-free,
if gluten-free chocolate
is used

Makes 20
Prep: 15 mins
Chill: 30 mins

50g/2oz/⅓ cup dark (bittersweet) chocolate, broken into pieces

85g/3⅓oz/4 Medjool dates, stoned (pitted)

150g/5oz/1 carton French-style soft goat's cheese (without rind)

25g/1oz/¼ cup unsweetened desiccated (dry shredded) coconut, plus 2 tbsp/30ml to decorate

2 tbsp/30ml cacao powder

2 tbsp/30ml plain soya protein powder

1 tbsp/15ml maple syrup

1 tsp/5ml vanilla extract

½ tsp/2.5ml ground cinnamon

2 tbsp/30ml grated chocolate

2 tbsp/30ml cranberries, finely chopped

Energy 89kcal/371kJ; Protein 3.6g; Carbohydrate 7.4g, of which sugars 7.1g; Fat 5.1g, of which saturates 3.7g; Cholesterol 7mg; Calcium 17mg; Fibre 1.2g; Sodium 61mg.

Minted matcha & almond balls

Vegan
Dairy-free
Gluten-free
No added sugar

Makes 20
Prep: 10 mins

20 large mint leaves

1 tsp/5ml matcha tea blend or the contents of 1 matcha tea bag

1 tbsp/15ml dried sea salad

3 tbsp/45ml hemp powder

2 tbsp/30ml pumpkin seed butter

75g/3oz/½ cup unblanched almonds

75g/3oz/4 ready-to-eat dried pear halves or 6 dried apricots

50g/2oz/generous ½ cup unsweetened desiccated (dry shredded) coconut

Grated zest and juice of 1 lemon

2 tbsp/30ml unsweetened almond milk or water

1 tsp/5ml hemp or moringa powder to finish (optional)

These fresh-tasting power balls are refreshingly moist with the clean zingy flavour of mint and lemon combined with antioxidant-rich Japanese matcha tea.

1 Add the mint leaves, matcha tea, sea salad and hemp powder to a food processor then add the seed butter, almonds and pear or apricots and blitz until finely chopped.

2 Add the coconut, lemon zest and juice, and milk or water, and blend again until the mixture begins to clump together.

3 Squeeze the mixture into a ball, take out of the processor bowl and cut into 20 pieces. Roll each piece in the palm of your hands to make a smooth ball then roll in hemp or moringa powder, if liked.

4 Pack into a plastic container, interleaving the layers with baking parchment. Store in the refrigerator for up to 3 days.

Energy 66kcal/273kJ; Protein 1.9g; Carbohydrate 3.3g, of which sugars 2g; Fat 5.1g, of which saturates 1.8g; Cholesterol 0mg; Calcium 13mg; Fibre 1.8g; Sodium 11mg.

Gingered beet & blackberry balls

Dairy-free
Vegan
No added sugar

Makes 16
Prep: 15 mins

85g/3⅓oz/4 Medjool dates, stones (pitted)

110g/4oz/1 cup porridge (rolled) oats

50g/2oz/⅓ cup unblanched almonds

15g/½oz/small piece fresh root ginger, peeled and chopped

75g/3oz/1 small trimmed beetroot (beet), peeled and coarsely grated

50g/2oz/⅓ cup frozen blackberries

COOK'S TIP If you don't have fresh root ginger then add ½ tsp/2.5ml ground ginger instead.

These vibrant deep purple power balls pack an energising punch. Keep a pack of blackberries in the freezer and just take out a few when you need them; the beetroot will happily sit for a week or so in the vegetable drawer of the refrigerator, ready for action.

1 Add the dates, oats, almonds and ginger to a food processor and blitz together until finely chopped.

2 Add the beetroot and frozen blackberries and blitz again until the mixture begins to clump together.

3 Squeeze the mixture together, take out of the processor bowl and cut into 16 pieces. Roll each piece in the palm of your hands to make a smooth ball. Pack into a plastic container, interleaving the layers with baking parchment. Store in the refrigerator for up to 3 days.

NUTRITION TIP Blackberries and beetroot get their very deep colour from the antioxidant group of betalains. Plus, they contain vitamin C to boost the immune system, folates for new cell growth and DNA plus fibre.

Energy 64kcal/268kJ; Protein 1.8g; Carbohydrate 9.4g, of which sugars 4.2g; Fat 2.4g, of which saturates 0.1g; Cholesterol 0mg; Calcium 16mg; Fibre 1.2g; Sodium 6mg.

Mixed seed power balls

Packed with super-healthy fibre, minerals, protein and natural fruit sugars, these nutrient-dense bites will give you a slow sustained energy boost.

1 Add the millet to a food processor and blend until a fine powder. Add the figs, dates, cinnamon, vanilla and soya protein. Blend until a smooth paste forms.

2 Add the seeds and soya milk, and blend briefly so that the seeds are left in chunky pieces and the mixture is beginning to clump together.

3 Squeeze the mixture together, take out of the processor bowl and cut into 20 pieces. Roll each piece in the palm of your hands to make a smooth ball.

4 Pack into a plastic container, interleaving the layers with baking parchment. Store in the refrigerator for up to 3 days.

NUTRITION TIP Even if you don't go to the gym, you still need protein, especially as you age, for the maintenance and repair of every cell in your body and to help maintain muscle strength.
COOK'S TIP If you don't have any millet flakes then use buckwheat flakes or (checking the product if you are on a gluten-free diet), oats.

Nut-free
Dairy-free
Gluten-free
No added sugar

Makes 20
Prep: 10 mins

75g/3oz/½ cup millet flakes
100g/3¾oz/4 ready-to-eat
dried figs, sliced
50g/2oz/4 Medjool dates,
stoned (pitted)
1 tsp/5ml ground cinnamon
1 tsp/5ml vanilla extract
3 tbsp/45ml soya protein
powder
2 tbsp/30ml pumpkin seeds
2 tbsp/30ml sunflower seeds
1 tbsp/15ml chia seeds
1 tbsp/15ml hulled hemp
seeds
3 tbsp/45ml unsweetened
soya milk

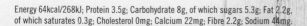

Energy 64kcal/268kJ; Protein 3.5g; Carbohydrate 8g, of which sugars 5.3g; Fat 2.2g,
of which saturates 0.3g; Cholesterol 0mg; Calcium 22mg; Fibre 2.2g; Sodium 44mg.

Chocolate brownie balls

Dairy-free
Vegan
No added sugar

Makes 20
Prep: 15 mins

100g/3¾oz unblanched hazelnuts

100g/3¾oz/¾ cup porridge (rolled) oats

150g/5oz/8 Medjool dates, stoned (pitted)

4 tbsp/60ml cacao powder

2 tbsp/30ml ground flaxseeds

2 tbsp/30ml soya protein powder

3 tbsp/45ml light olive oil

3–4 tbsp/45–60ml unsweetened almond milk

2 tbsp/30ml dried goji berries, finely chopped (optional)

All the flavour of chocolate brownies and chocolate spread in a power ball, the only sweetness coming from naturally sweet high-fibre dates rather than refined sugar, so great for kids and adults too.

1 Add the hazelnuts to a frying pan and cook over a medium heat for 2–3 minutes, shaking the pan until the nuts are evenly browned. Alternatively grill or broil on a piece of foil if preferred. Wrap in a kitchen towel and rub off the skins.

2 Add the toasted hazelnuts and oats to a food processor and blitz until finely chopped. Add the dates, cacao powder, flaxseeds, protein powder, oil and milk. Blitz until finely chopped and the mixture is beginning to clump together.

3 Squeeze the mixture into a ball, take out of the processor and cut into 20 pieces. Roll each piece in the palm of your hands to make a smooth ball then roll the balls in chopped goji berries, if liked. Pack into a plastic container, interleaving the layers with baking parchment. Store in the refrigerator for up to 3 days.

NUTRITION TIP The date palm has been around since Stone Age times. Medjool dates are fresh dates and contain half the calories of dried dates. Naturally sweet they are also a good source of soluble dietary fibre which means that the sugar is released slowly by the body for a sustained energy-boost.

Energy 110kcal/461kJ; Protein 3.7g; Carbohydrate 10g, of which sugars 5.3g; Fat 6.4g, of which saturates 0.9g; Cholesterol 0mg; Calcium 17mg; Fibre 2.4g; Sodium 37mg.

Very berry energy balls

School-age children seem to grow at an incredible rate, yet many can have small appetites. Power balls can be a great way to boost protein levels in a nutrient-dense, easy snackable way.

1 Add the oats to a food processor and blitz until finely chopped. Add the protein powder, flaxseeds, oil and honey then spoon in the raspberries and blend together until smooth.

2 Add the cranberries, goji berries and 1 tbsp/15ml milk and blend briefly until chunky pieces of dried fruit are still visible and the mixture has begun to clump together. Add more milk if needed.

3 Squeeze the mixture into a ball, take out of the processor and cut into 18 pieces. Roll each piece in the palm of your hands to make a smooth ball. Pack into a plastic container, interleaving the layers with baking parchment. Store in the refrigerator for up to 3 days.

COOK'S TIP If your kids hate bits then just blitz a little longer in the food processor so that the mixture becomes smooth.

Nut-free
Dairy-free

Makes 18
Prep: 10 mins

150g/5oz/1½ cups porridge (rolled) oats

3 tbsp/45ml soya protein powder

2 tbsp/30ml ground flaxseeds

2 tbsp/30ml light olive oil

1 tbsp/15ml clear honey

100g/3¾oz/scant 1 cup raspberries

2 tbsp/30ml dried cranberries

2 tbsp/30ml dried goji berries

1–2 tbsp/15–30ml unsweetened soya milk

NUTRITION TIP Raspberries are a good source of vitamin C, needed daily to boost our immune system, plus they also contain manganese which helps with the metabolism of carbs and protein.

Energy 75kcal/315kJ; Protein 3.6g; Carbohydrate 10g, of which sugars 3.2g; Fat 2.5g, of which saturates 0.2g; Cholesterol 0mg; Calcium 8mg; Fibre 1.8g; Sodium 9mg.

Apricot & coconut balls

Dairy-free
Vegan
Gluten-free
No added sugar

Makes 20
Prep: 10 mins

75g/3oz/½ cup cashew nut pieces

75g/3oz/¾ cup unsweetened desiccated (dry shredded) coconut

2 tbsp/30ml hulled hemp seeds

50g/2oz/½ cup buckwheat flakes

150g/5oz/scant 1 cup ready-to-eat dried apricots

125ml/4fl oz/¼ cup unsweetened almond milk

A little extra unsweetened desiccated (dry shredded) coconut, for rolling (optional)

These bright yellow power balls are made with ready-to-eat dried apricots and creamy smooth cashew nuts, for a natural sweet fix that is a much healthier and more nutrient-dense alternative to munching on a store-bought snack.

1 Add the cashew nuts, coconut, hemp seeds and buckwheat flakes to a food processor and blitz until a fine powder.

2 Add the apricots and nut milk and blitz again until the mixture is very smooth and beginning to clump together.

3 Squeeze the mixture into a ball, take out of the processor and cut into 20 pieces. Roll each piece in the palm of your hands to make a smooth ball.

4 Roll in a little extra coconut, if liked, then pack into a plastic container, interleaving the layers with baking parchment. Store in the refrigerator for up to 3 days.

NUTRITION TIP Hemp seeds are rich in omega-3 and -6 essential fatty acids and are a good source of protein.
COOK'S TIP If you don't have any buckwheat flakes then just use porridge (rolled) oats instead, if not on a special diet.

Energy 73kcal/303kJ; Protein 1.8g; Carbohydrate 6g, of which sugars 3.8g; Fat 4.8g, of which saturates 2.4g; Cholesterol 0mg; Calcium 9mg; Fibre 2.5g; Sodium 31mg.

Red velvet bites

Forget about baking, these mini naturally-sweet snacks have all the flavour of red velvet cake but can be made in just a few minutes.

1 Add the dates, oats, hemp seeds and desiccated coconut to a food processor and blitz until finely chopped.

2 Add the grated beetroot, cacao powder, cashew nut butter and coconut oil then spoon in the almond milk and blitz together until smooth and beginning to clump together.

3 Squeeze into a ball, remove from the food processor and cut into 20 pieces. Roll each piece in the palm of your hands to make a ball then lightly dust with a little extra cacao. Pack into a plastic container, interleaving the layers with baking parchment. Store in the refrigerator for up to 3 days.

Dairy-free
Vegan
No added sugar

Makes 20
Prep: 15 mins

110g/4oz/5 Medjool dates, stoned (pitted)

110g/4oz/1 cup porridge (rolled) oats

2 tbsp/30ml hulled hemp seeds

50g/2oz/½ cup unsweetened desiccated (dry shredded) coconut

75g/3oz/1 small trimmed beetroot (beet), peeled and coarsely grated

2 tbsp/30ml cacao powder, plus extra for dusting

2 tbsp/30ml smooth cashew nut butter

1 tbsp/15ml coconut oil

4 tbsp/60ml unsweetened almond milk

NUTRITION TIP Coconuts are not actually a true nut at all but a drupe or a one-seeded dry drupe if being really precise. Some people who are allergic to tree nuts like almonds, cashews and walnuts may also be allergic to coconut, so before introducing to your diet check with your health professional. Every bit of the coconut can be used and is sometimes called the 'tree of life' as you can drink the water from the centre, eat the flesh, use the shell for bowls and the outside fibre as fuel.
COOK'S TIP Beetroot does tend to stain your hands and chopping board so make sure to wash well straight after use. You may prefer to wear disposable plastic gloves when grating or whizz the beetroot through the food processor with the grated disc attachment and then scoop out with a spoon on to a plate until ready to mix.

Energy 80kcal/335kJ; Protein 2g; Carbohydrate 9.3g, of which sugars 4.2g; Fat 4.2g, of which saturates 2.2g; Cholesterol 0mg; Calcium 9mg; Fibre 2.2g; Sodium 26mg.

Summer berry & minted yogurt balls

No added sugar

Makes 20

Prep: 10 mins

110g/4oz/1 cup porridge
(rolled) oats

75g/3oz/1 cup quinoa flakes

150g/5oz/1 cup cashew nuts

3 tbsp/45ml sunflower seeds

150g/5oz/1 cup frozen mixed
summer berries, no need to
defrost

4 tbsp/60ml natural (plain)
low-fat yogurt

20 mint leaves

A little unsweetened
desiccated (dry shredded)
coconut, for rolling (optional)

Frozen summer berries make an immune-boosting vitamin C-packed standby ingredient for these summery-tasting power balls. Great for kids too.

1 Add the oats, quinoa flakes, nuts and sunflower seeds to a food processor and blitz together until a fine powder.

2 Spoon in the frozen berries, yogurt and mint leaves and blitz again until well mixed and smooth.

3 Scoop the mixture out of the food processor, shape into a ball (this mixture is a little softer than some of the other power balls) then cut into 20 pieces. Roll each piece in the palm of your hand to make a ball.

4 Roll the balls in a little coconut if liked then pack into a plastic container, interleaving the layers with baking parchment. Store in the refrigerator for up to 2 days.

COOK'S TIP As these power balls contain yogurt, pack into a plastic box with a mini frozen ice block to keep cold or add to an insulated lunch bag to keep them chilled when out and about.

NUTRITION TIP Protein levels are boosted with the quinoa flakes and sunflower seeds; these are finely ground in the food processor before adding the other ingredients so that you don't even notice that they are there.

Energy 94kcal/393kJ; Protein 3.1g; Carbohydrate 9.1g, of which sugars 1.8g; Fat 5.3g, of which saturates 0.9g; Cholesterol 0mg; Calcium 17mg; Fibre 1.9g; Sodium 35mg.

Super fruity power balls

These power balls store well in the refrigerator or freezer. Simply take out as many as you need in the morning and they should be defrosted by mid-morning for a healthy nutrient-boosting snack.

1 Add the buckwheat flakes and almonds to a food processor and blitz until finely ground.

2 Add the almond butter, sunflower seeds and dried fruits then spoon in the orange juice. Blitz briefly until the mixture just begins to clump together and the dried fruits are still in chunky pieces.

3 Squeeze the mixture together, take out of the processor bowl and cut into 20 pieces. Roll each piece in the palm of your hands to make a smooth ball. Pack into a plastic container, interleaving the layers with baking parchment. Store in the refrigerator for up to 3 days.

COOK'S TIP Make sure to very finely chop the sunflower seeds along with the nuts and buckwheat flakes if making for children younger than 7.

Gluten-free
Dairy-free
Vegan
No added sugar

Makes 20

Prep: 10 mins

110g/4oz/1 cup buckwheat flakes

50g/2oz/⅓ cup unblanched almonds

2 tbsp/30ml almond nut butter

3 tbsp/45ml sunflower seeds

110g/4oz/generous ½ cup mixed dried cranberries, goji berries, diced mango and diced ready-to-eat apricots, or mix of dried fruits of your choice

Juice of 1 medium orange

Energy 67kcal/281kJ; Protein 2.1g; Carbohydrate 7.1g, of which sugars 3.6g; Fat 3.6g, of which saturates 0.4g; Cholesterol 0mg; Calcium 15mg; Fibre 1.8g; Sodium 45mg.

Blueberry & chia balls

Blueberries are a great source of immune-boosting vitamin C and vitamin K and are packed with cancer-fighting antioxidants along with the mineral manganese which helps process cholesterol, carbohydrates, protein and phenolic compounds. No wonder they are often called a superfood.

1 Add the oats and cashew nut pieces to a food processor and blitz until very finely chopped.

2 Spoon in the protein powder, chia seeds and cashew butter. Add the blueberries, lemon zest and juice and acai powder if using. Blitz together until the blueberries are finely chopped and the mixture is beginning to clump together.

3 Squeeze the mixture into a ball, take out of the processor and cut into 20 pieces. Roll each piece in the palm of your hands to make a smooth ball. Press a whole blueberry into the top of each power ball. Sprinkle with acai powder, if liked.

4 Pack into a plastic container, interleaving the layers with baking parchment and store in the refrigerator for up to 2 days.

COOK'S TIP If you make your own cashew milk then use a little of the soaked cashews in this recipe, adding to the food processor after the oats have been finely ground.

These have no added sugar but for those with a very sweet tooth, add a teaspoon or two of honey or maple syrup or your preferred sweetener.

Dairy-free
Vegan
No added sugar

Makes 20
Prep: 15 mins

100g/3¾oz/¾ cups porridge (rolled) oats
75g/3oz/½ cup cashew nut pieces
3 tbsp/45ml soya protein powder
2 tbsp/30ml chia seeds
1 tbsp/15ml cashew nut butter
110g/4oz/¾ cup blueberries, plus 20 extra to decorate
Grated zest and juice of 1 lemon
1 tsp/5ml acai powder (optional)

Energy 64kcal/267kJ; Protein 3.6g; Carbohydrate 5.5g, of which sugars 0.8g; Fat 3.2g, of which saturates 0.5g; Cholesterol 0mg; Calcium 11mg; Fibre 1.6g; Sodium 17mg.

Fig & tahini energy balls

Nut-free
Dairy-free
Gluten-free
No added sugar

Makes 20
Prep: 10 mins

110g/4oz/1 cup buckwheat flakes

75g/3oz/4 ready-to-eat dried figs

4cm/1½in piece fresh root ginger, sliced

2 tbsp/30ml tahini

2 tsp/10ml spirulina powder

1 tbsp/15ml dried sea salad

3 tbsp/45ml unsweetened soya milk

Packed with fibre and natural fruit sugars, ready-to-eat dried figs make a great store cupboard alternative to fresh Medjool dates and mixed with spirulina and sea salad they become the most incredibly dark, almost Halloween-style power balls that are bursting with essential minerals.

1 Add the buckwheat flakes, figs and ginger to a food processor and blend until very finely chopped.

2 Add the tahini, spirulina and sea salad then the soya milk, blend until well mixed and beginning to clump together.

3 Squeeze the mixture into a ball, take out of the food processor and cut into 20 pieces. Roll each piece in the palm of your hands to make a smooth ball. Pack into a plastic container, interleaving the layers with baking parchment. Store in the refrigerator for up to 3 days.

COOK'S TIP Tahini is a Mediterranean-style sesame paste, most often used in hummus but it can also be added to recipes in place of a nut butter. Buy in glass jars.

Energy 35kcal/149kJ; Protein 1g; Carbohydrate 5.9g, of which sugars 3.2g; Fat 1g, of which saturates 0.1g; Cholesterol 0mg; Calcium 12mg; Fibre 1.2g; Sodium 47mg.

Orange & puffed rice amazeballs

Nut-free

Makes 16
Prep: 10 mins

1 clementine, peeled and segments roughly separated

100g/3¾oz/4 Medjool dates, stoned (pitted)

2 tbsp/30ml sesame seeds

2 tbsp/30ml soya protein powder

2 tbsp/30ml pumpkin seed butter

½ tsp/2.5ml ground turmeric

½ tsp/2.5ml ground cinnamon

½ tsp/2.5ml vanilla extract

2 tsp/5ml maple syrup

40g/1½oz/1½ cups plain puffed rice

A little cacao powder, for dusting (optional)

While we should all be watching our sugar intake, it is important to think about where the sugar comes from. Encourage the family to go for snacks such as this healthy rice-based one made with naturally sweet dates and just a tiny touch of maple syrup – to boost energy levels, aid concentration and help maintain a balance of blood sugar.

1 Add the clementine and dates to a food processor and blitz until very finely chopped.

2 Spoon in the sesame seeds, protein powder, seed butter and spices then the vanilla and maple syrup. Blitz again until smooth.

3 Spoon in the puffed rice and mix very briefly together until the puffed rice is only just beginning to break into pieces and the mixture is clumping together.

4 Squeeze the mixture into a ball, take out of the processor and then cut into 16 pieces. Wet your hands then roll each piece in the palm of your hands to make a smooth ball.

5 Dust with a little cacao powder, if liked. Pack into a plastic container, interleaving the layers with baking parchment, and store in the refrigerator for up to 2 days.

NUTRITIONAL TIP Spices and vanilla extract add flavour and give the sensation of sweetness to help mask the lack of added sugar. COOK'S TIP Look out for bags of plain puffed rice in the health food store; don't get it confused with the very sweet sugared breakfast cereal which is actually puffed wheat.

Energy 57kcal/241kJ; Protein 2.6g; Carbohydrate 7.6g, of which sugars 4.9g; Fat 2.1g, of which saturates 0.4g; Cholesterol 0mg; Calcium 28mg; Fibre 0.7g; Sodium 17mg.

MUESLI BARS

While we all like to think that muesli or flapjack style bars are healthy, many recipes contain large amounts of butter and sugar. Made with a mixture of wholegrains such as oats, buckwheat flakes or quinoa flakes they add fibre, help to reduce cholesterol and in the case of quinoa add protein too. The recipes in this chapter are all made with much less sugar and butter than traditional recipes, with lots of options to use dairy-free soya margarine or olive oil too. Flavour has been added with naturally sweet dried fruits, spices, orange zest and juice, and vanilla extract.

Banana & cranberry muesli bars

Nut-free

Cuts into 14
Prep: 15 mins
Cook: 20–25 mins

100g/3¾oz/scant ½ cup
butter
100g/3¾oz/generous ½ cup
light muscovado (brown)
sugar
225g/8oz/2½ cups porridge
(rolled) oats
150g/5oz/1 medium banana,
unpeeled weight
3 tbsp/45ml ground flaxseeds
3 tbsp/45ml dried cranberries

Naturally sweet, bananas are a favourite fruit; don't throw away a banana from the fruit bowl that is a little brown and speckled, mash it and add to these fresh fruity muesli bars instead.

1 Preheat the oven to 180°C/350°F/Gas 4. Cut a piece of baking parchment a little larger than an 18 x 28 x 4cm/7 x 11 x 1½in rectangular tin or pan, snip into the corners then press into the tin so that the base and sides are lined with paper.

2 Add the butter and sugar to a pan and warm together until the sugar has dissolved. Add the oats and cook, stirring for a minute or two until just beginning to soften, then take off the heat.

3 Peel and mash the banana on a plate then stir into the oat mixture along with the flaxseeds and cranberries.

4 Tip into the lined tin, press flat and bake for 20 minutes until browned. Leave to cool in the tin for 10 minutes then mark into bars and leave to cool completely.

5 Lift the paper and bars out of the tin, peel off the paper and cut right through into bars. Pack into a plastic container and store for up to 3 days.

COOK'S TIP If your kids aren't fans of cranberries then add a handful of sultanas (golden raisins) or diced chocolate instead.

For a dairy-free or vegan diet, swap the butter for soya margarine.

Energy 181kcal/761kJ; Protein 3g; Carbohydrate 25.1g, of which sugars 12g; Fat 8.3g, of which saturates 3.8g; Cholesterol 15mg; Calcium 15mg; Fibre 3g; Sodium 59mg.

Dairy-free
Vegan
Nut-free

Cuts into 10
Prep: 20 mins
Cook: 25–30 mins

110g/4oz/scant ¾ cup dried apricots
125ml/4fl oz/½ cup water
100g/3¾oz/½ cup soya margarine
50g/2oz/¼ cup light muscovado (brown) sugar
50g/2oz/⅓ cup maple syrup
225g/8oz/2 cups barley flakes
Juice of 1 medium orange
2 tbsp/30ml ground flaxseeds
3 tbsp/45ml sunflower seeds

Triple decker with apricot

Bite through the crunchy sunflower seed topping to a ribbon of naturally sweet apricot purée and down to a crisp flapjack base. A perfect energising pick-me-up with a cup of tea mid-afternoon or with a glass of milk as an after-school snack for the kids.

1 Preheat the oven to 180°C/350°F/Gas 4. Cut a square of baking parchment a little larger than a 20cm/8in shallow square cake tin or pan, snip into the corners then press the paper into the tin so that the base and sides are lined.

2 Add the apricots and water to a small pan, bring to the boil then simmer for about 5 minutes until soft. Take off the heat. Purée in a food processor or liquidizer until smooth.

3 Add the margarine, sugar and maple syrup to a medium pan and heat until just melted. Add the barley flakes and orange juice and cook, stirring, over a low heat for a few minutes to soften the barley flakes.

4 Stir in the ground flaxseeds then tip three-quarters of the barley mixture into the lined tin and press flat. Spoon the apricot purée on top and spread into an even layer. Mix the sunflower seeds into the remaining barley, scatter over the top and lightly press down into the apricot purée.

5 Bake for 20–25 minutes until the topping is golden brown. Leave to cool for 10 minutes then mark into 10 bars and leave to cool completely.

6 Remove the bars and paper from the tin, cut right through then lift off the paper and pack into a plastic container. Store in the refrigerator for up to 2 days.

NUTRITION TIP Drying fresh apricots concentrates the amounts of beta-carotene, potassium and iron in the fruit but does also concentrate sugar levels. They are a good source of fibre.

Energy 262kcal/1096kJ; Protein 4.9g; Carbohydrate 32.1g, of which sugars 13.6g; Fat 13.4g, of which saturates 2.1g; Cholesterol 0mg; Calcium 33mg; Fibre 4.7g; Sodium 92mg.

Choc-dipped quinoa bars

Gluten-free,
if gluten-free chocolate
is used
Nut-free

Cuts into 12
Prep: 15 mins
Cook: 15–20 mins

50g/2oz/¼ cup butter
2 tbsp/30ml sunflower oil
2 tbsp/30ml clear honey
2 tbsp/30ml molasses sugar
2 tbsp/30ml ground flaxseeds
100g/3¾oz/1 cup quinoa
flakes
110g/4oz/1 cup buckwheat
flakes
50g/2oz/⅓ cup golden or
brown sultanas (golden
raisins)
1 tsp/5ml vanilla extract
1 egg white
100g/3¾oz/1 bar dark
chocolate, broken into
pieces

These tasty super-chocolatey bars are a great pre-workout or after-school energy boost to munch on.

1 Preheat the oven to 180°C/350°F/Gas 4. Cut a square of baking parchment a little larger than a 20cm/8in shallow square cake tin or pan, snip diagonally into the corners then press the paper into the tin so that the base and sides are lined.

2 Add the butter, oil, honey and molasses sugar to a medium pan and heat gently, stirring until the sugar has melted. Stir in the ground flaxseeds, quinoa and buckwheat flakes and cook, stirring for a minute or two to soften the buckwheat. Mix in the sultanas and vanilla.

3 Lightly beat the egg white with a fork until frothy then stir into the muesli bar mix. Tip into the lined tin and press into an even layer with the back of a fork. Bake for 15–20 minutes until browned.

4 Leave to cool for 10 minutes then mark into bars. Lift out of the tin, peel away the paper and cut into 12 pieces.

5 Melt the chocolate in a bowl set over a pan of gently simmering water, then one at a time, dip each end of a muesli bar into the chocolate and put on to a baking sheet lined with baking parchment. Repeat until all the bars have been dipped. Chill in the refrigerator until the chocolate is firm then pack into a plastic container, interleaving with more baking parchment. Store in the refrigerator for up to 3 days.

NUTRITION TIP Quinoa has been growing in popularity as it is one of the few grains to contain all the essential amino acids that make up the building blocks of protein. We all need protein for growth and repair of muscle tissue as well as building enzymes, hormones and antibodies to boost our immune system, but it is even more important for growing kids.

Energy 190kcal/796kJ; Protein 3g; Carbohydrate 25.5g, of which sugars 12.7g; Fat 9.1g, of which saturates 3.8g; Cholesterol 9mg; Calcium 17mg; Fibre 2g; Sodium 38mg.

Multi-grain & molasses bars

These muesli bars are not only thin and crispy, with a snap when you break them, but are made with only a small amount of unsaturated oil and sweetened with just a little treacle-like molasses sugar and maple syrup.

1 Preheat the oven to 180°C/350°F/Gas 4. Cut a piece of baking parchment a little larger than a 20cm/8in shallow square cake tin or pan, snip into the corners then press the paper into the tin so that the base and sides are lined.

2 Add the oil, molasses sugar and maple syrup to a pan and warm together until the molasses has dissolved. Stir in the oats, barley and rye, then the sesame seeds, and cook, stirring for a minute or two to soften slightly.

3 Lightly whisk the egg white with a fork until frothy then stir into the grain mixture. Tip into the paper-lined tin and press flat with the back of a fork.

4 Bake for 15–20 minutes until browned. Leave to cool in the tin for 10 minutes then mark into 10 bars and leave to cool completely.

5 Lift the paper and bars out of the tin, peel away the paper and cut right through into bars. Pack into a plastic container and store for up to 3 days.

NUTRITION TIP Sesame seeds are a good source of vitamin E and calcium. Along with other seeds and nuts, they also contain omega-3 and omega-6 fatty acids, although the best source of this is fish. If you don't like or don't eat much fish then adding more nuts and seeds to snacks can be a great and easy way to boost your daily intake. COOK'S TIP If you don't have the three types of grains then mix and match using what you do have to make up a total of 100g/3¾oz/¾ cup, or use all porridge (rolled) oats if preferred.

**Dairy-free
Nut-free**

Cuts into 10
Prep: 15 mins
Cook: 15–20 mins

4 tbsp/60ml sunflower oil
4 tbsp/60ml molasses sugar
2 tbsp/30ml maple syrup
50g/2oz/½ cup porridge
(rolled) oats
25g/1oz/¼ cup barley flakes
25g/1oz/¼ cup rye flakes
3 tbsp/45ml sesame seeds
1 egg white

Energy 127kcal/530kJ; Protein 2.4g; Carbohydrate 12.3g, of which sugars 4.8g; Fat 7.9g, of which saturates 1g; Cholesterol 0mg; Calcium 62mg; Fibre 1.4g; Sodium 19mg.

Super-seedy buckwheat bars

Traditionally made with oats, muesli-style bars also taste great with buckwheat flakes instead, readily available in the health food shop, and they are gluten- and wheat-free too.

1 Preheat the oven to 180°C/350°F/Gas 4. Cut a piece of baking parchment a little larger than an 18 x 28 x 4cm/7 x 11 x 1½in rectangular tin or pan, snip into the corners then press the paper into the tin so that the base and sides are lined.

2 Add the butter, sugar and honey to a pan and warm together until the butter and sugar have dissolved. Stir in the buckwheat flakes and seeds and cook, stirring for a minute or two to slightly soften.

3 Lightly whisk the egg white with a fork until frothy then stir into the seed mix. Tip into the paper-lined tin and press flat with the back of a fork.

4 Bake for 20 minutes until browned. Leave to cool in the tin for 10 minutes then mark into 12 bars and leave to cool completely. Lift the paper and bars out of the tin, peel away the paper and cut right through into bars. Pack into a plastic container and eat within 3 days.

Gluten-free Nut-free

Cuts into 12
Prep: 15 mins
Cook: 20 mins

100g/3¾oz/scant ½ cup butter
50g/2oz/¼ cup light muscovado (brown) sugar
3 tbsp/45ml honey
175g/6oz/scant 2 cups buckwheat flakes
110g/4oz/1 cup mixed seeds, to include hulled hemp, sesame, pumpkin and sunflower seeds
1 egg white

COOK'S TIP Buy buckwheat flakes in packs from the health food store, it looks just like small porridge (rolled) oats; although gluten-free, always check the pack before buying as some grains can be contaminated with wheat during processing. If you are not on a special diet then you might like to use porridge oats instead.

If you are following a vegan diet swap the honey for maple syrup or a sweetener of your choice and use soya margarine rather than butter.

Energy 195kcal/817kJ; Protein 4.1g; Carbohydrate 21.2g, of which sugars 7.5g; Fat 11g, of which saturates 4.6g; Cholesterol 18mg; Calcium 11mg; Fibre 5g; Sodium 89mg.

Pumpkin seed, almond & cherry bars

Dairy-free

Cuts into 14
Prep: 15 mins
Cook: 20–25 mins

150g/5oz/10 tbsp soya margarine
3 tbsp/45ml clear honey
2 tbsp/30ml molasses syrup
2 tbsp/30ml barley malt extract
225g/8oz/2 cups porridge (rolled) oats
40g/1½oz/⅓ cup self-raising (self-rising) flour
75g/3oz/½ cup pumpkin seeds
75g/3oz/½ cup unblanched almonds, halved
50g/2oz/⅓ cup dried sour cherries

Wrap bars individually in baking parchment or foil so that they are easy to grab in the morning, an energy-boosting snack-to-go at a fraction of the cost of store-bought.

1 Preheat the oven to 180°C/350°F/Gas 4. Cut a piece of baking parchment a little larger than an 18 x 28 x 4cm/7 x 11 x 1½in rectangular tin or pan, snip into the corners then press the paper into the tin so that the base and sides are lined.

2 Add the margarine, honey, molasses and malt extract to a pan and warm together until the margarine has melted. Take the pan off the heat and stir in the oats and flour then mix in the seeds, almonds and cherries.

3 Tip into the lined tin, press flat with a fork and bake for 20–25 minutes until browned. Leave to cool in the tin for 10 minutes then mark into bars and leave to cool completely.

4 Lift the paper and bars out of the tin, peel off the paper and cut right through into 14 bars. Pack into a plastic container and store for up to 3 days.

COOK'S TIP If you don't have any sour cherries then use dried cranberries instead.
NUTRITION TIP It can be hard to cut out sugar in one go, so try to gradually reduce the amount that you consume. Start by cutting out fizzy drinks and ready-made cakes, biscuits and cookies that have little or no added nutritional value. Then once you have got the family round to eating healthy wholegrains begin to reduce the amount of sugar in these too.

Energy 247kcal/1032kJ; Protein 4.8g; Carbohydrate 22.9g, of which sugars 8.1g; Fat 15.8g, of which saturates 2.4g; Cholesterol 0mg; Calcium 60mg; Fibre 2.1g; Sodium 99mg.

Nut bonanza bars

Full of protein-packed nuts and peanut butter, these bars make the perfect snack to take to the gym to munch on pre- or post-workout.

1 Preheat the oven to 180°C/350°F/Gas 4. Cut a piece of baking parchment a little larger than an 18 x 28 x 4cm/7 x 11 x 1½in rectangular tin or pan, snip into the corners then press the paper into the tin so that base and sides are lined.

2 Add the margarine, peanut butter, sugar and maple syrup to a pan and warm together until the sugar has dissolved. Stir in the oats and milk and cook for 2–3 minutes, stirring until the oats have softened. Stir in the nuts.

3 Tip the mixture into the paper-lined tin and press flat. Bake for 20 minutes until browned. Leave to cool in the tin for 10 minutes then mark into 14 bars and leave to cool completely.

4 Lift the paper and bars out of the tin, peel away the paper and cut right through into bars. Pack into a plastic container and store for up to 3 days.

NUTRITION NOTE Nuts not only contain protein but essential fatty acids, useful amounts of B vitamins and minerals. Just 1 brazil nut contains an adult's daily requirement of the mineral selenium, that helps to protect the body from free radical damage and is a difficult mineral to obtain on a vegan diet.
COOK'S TIP These bars are made with chunky pieces of nut, if you would like to serve these to kids then chop the nuts into smaller pieces or blitz in a food processor. Always check with the parent of a visiting child about the possibility of nut allergy before offering these healthy bars.

Dairy-free
Vegan

Cuts into 14
Prep: 15 mins
Cook: 20 mins

100g/3¾oz/scant ½ cup soya margarine

75g/3oz/⅓ cup crunchy peanut butter

75g/3oz/6 tbsp light muscovado (brown) sugar

2 tbsp/30ml maple syrup

200g/7oz/2 cups porridge (rolled) oats

125ml/4fl oz/½ cup unsweetened almond milk

110g/4oz/1 cup mixed unblanched almonds, unblanched hazelnuts and brazil nuts, roughly chopped or nuts of choice

Energy 219kcal/914kJ; Protein 4.7g; Carbohydrate 18.7g, of which sugars 7.6g; Fat 14.4g, of which saturates 2.3g; Cholesterol 0mg; Calcium 32mg; Fibre 1.3g; Sodium 80mg.

Nectarine & coconut muesli bars

**Dairy-free
Vegan**

Cuts into 10
Prep: 20 mins
Cook: 20–25 mins

100g/3¾oz/scant ½ cup soya margarine
100g/3¾oz/generous ½ cup light muscovado (brown) sugar
225g/8oz/2 cups unsweetened fruit and nut muesli
40g/1½oz/⅓ cup unsweetened desiccated (dry shredded) coconut
50g/2oz/½ cup self-raising (self-rising) wholemeal (whole-wheat) flour
1 large nectarine, halved, stoned (pitted) and cut into small dice

You don't need many ingredients to make these tasty energy-boosting bars. Most of us have a bag of muesli in the cupboard. If you are not on a dairy-free diet then add butter instead of soya margarine and if you don't have a nectarine then add a finely diced apple or a couple of plums.

1 Preheat the oven to 180°C/350°F/Gas 4. Cut a square of baking parchment a little larger than a shallow 20cm/8in cake tin or pan. Snip diagonally into the corners then press the paper into the tin so that the base and sides are lined.

2 Add the margarine and sugar to a pan and heat, stirring until the sugar has dissolved.

3 Take the pan off the heat and stir in the muesli, two-thirds of the coconut, the flour and diced nectarine.

4 Tip into the lined tin, press down flat then sprinkle with the rest of the coconut. Bake for 20–25 minutes until the coconut is light browned. Leave to cool for 10 minutes then mark into 10 bars. Cool completely in the tin then cut into bars, lift off the paper and store in a plastic container for up to 3 days.

COOK'S TIP Ovens do vary and desiccated coconut can brown quickly so check on these muesli bars halfway through cooking and cover the top loosely with a sheet of foil if needed.

Energy 241kcal/1012kJ; Protein 3.5g; Carbohydrate 30.2g, of which sugars 15.5g; Fat 12.6g, of which saturates 4.2g; Cholesterol 0mg; Calcium 18mg; Fibre 3.8g; Sodium 81mg.

Tutti-frutti bars

These muesli bars are super-low in fat and added sugar with just 2 tablespoons of olive oil and 2 tbsp maple syrup and an optional sugar-sprinkle for the top. The sweetness comes from the chopped apple and dried fruits which are also a good source of minerals and fibre too.

1 Preheat the oven to 180°C/350°F/Gas 4. Cut a piece of baking parchment a little larger than an 18 x 28 x 4cm/7 x 11 x 1½in rectangular tin or pan, snip into the corners then press the paper into the tin so that the base and sides are lined.

2 Add the nuts to a food processor and finely chop. Add the apple and blitz until finely chopped then add the pumpkin and hemp seeds and mix briefly.

3 Heat the oil and maple syrup in a medium pan. Stir in the oats, cinnamon, dried fruit and almond milk and cook, stirring for 2–3 minutes until the oats have softened slightly.

4 Tip the mixture into the lined tin and press flat. Sprinkle with a little sugar if using. Bake for 25–30 minutes until golden brown. Leave to cool for 10 minutes then mark into bars and leave to cool.

5 Lift the paper and bars out of the tin, peel off the paper and cut the bars right through. Pack into a plastic container, and store for up to 3 days.

NUTRITIONAL TIP High-fibre oats and pectin-rich apples have been shown to help lower harmful cholesterol and to help regulate blood pressure. Apples also stimulate the growth of good bacteria in the large intestine.

COOK'S TIP Encouraging your family to cut down on sugar is best done gradually, that way they won't really notice. So try with less and less sugar sprinkled over the top and before long you will be able to leave it off altogether.

Dairy-free
Vegan

Cuts into 14
Prep: 25 mins
Cook: 25–30 mins

110g/4oz/1 cup mixed nuts, to include brazil nuts, cashew nut pieces, unblanched almonds or hazelnuts

1 apple, cored but not peeled and cut into chunks

3 tbsp/45ml pumpkin seeds

3 tbsp/45ml hulled hemp seeds

2 tbsp/30ml olive oil

2 tbsp/30ml maple syrup

225g/8oz/2 cups porridge (rolled) oats

1 tsp/5ml ground cinnamon

25g/1oz/2 tbsp dried cranberries

25g/1oz/2 tbsp dried cherries

50g/2oz ready-to-eat dried apricots, diced

250ml/8fl oz/1 cup unsweetened almond milk

2 tbsp/30ml demerara (raw) or light muscovado (brown) sugar (optional)

Energy 182kcal/763kJ; Protein 5.4g; Carbohydrate 18.7g, of which sugars 5g; Fat 10g, of which saturates 0.9g; Cholesterol 0mg; Calcium 33mg; Fibre 3.4g; Sodium 30mg.

Oatylicious blueberry & vanilla bars

Dairy-free
Nut-free

Cuts into 12
Prep: 2 mins
Cook: 25–30 mins

100g/3¾oz/scant ½ cup soya margarine

100g/3¾oz/generous ½ cup light muscovado (brown) sugar

100g/3¾oz/generous 1 cup quinoa flakes

110g/4oz/1 cup porridge (rolled) oats

Juice of 1 orange

50g/2oz/⅓ cup brown rice flour

1 tsp/5ml vanilla extract

1 egg white

150g/5oz/1 cup blueberries

2 tsp/10ml sesame seeds

Blueberries add little moist, juicy explosions as you bite into these healthy-wholegrain bars. Great to add to school lunch boxes or your gym bag.

1 Preheat the oven to 180°C/350°F/Gas 4. Cut a square of baking parchment a little larger than a 20cm/8in shallow square cake tin or pan, snip into the corners then press the paper into the tin so that the base and sides are lined.

2 Add the margarine and sugar to a pan and warm together until the sugar has dissolved. Stir in the quinoa flakes and oats then the orange juice and cook, stirring for a minute or two until the flakes and oats have softened slightly.

3 Take off the heat and mix in the rice flour and vanilla. Lightly beat the egg white in a bowl with a fork until frothy then stir into the oat mixture along with the blueberries.

4 Spoon into the paper lined tin, press flat, sprinkle over the sesame seeds and bake for 25–30 minutes until golden brown. Leave to cool in the tin for 10 minutes then mark into 12 bars.

5 Lift the paper and bars out of the tin, peel off the paper and cut right through into bars. Pack into a plastic container and store in the refrigerator for up to 3 days.

NUTRITION TIP Many teenagers tend to skip breakfast before school – these portable bars can be quickly packed into their school bag for a slow sustained energy-release that will not only help them to concentrate but may even improve their mental performance too.

Energy 195kcal/818kJ; Protein 2.9g; Carbohydrate 27.1g, of which sugars 10.4g; Fat 9g, of which saturates 1.5g; Cholesterol 0mg; Calcium 20mg; Fibre 2.2g; Sodium 69mg.

TRAYBAKE BITES

You don't need to stop eating cake just because you are trying to cut down the amount of sugar that you eat. Adding naturally sweet vegetables such as carrots, sweet potatoes and parsnips, or adding bananas or apples, helps to cut down the amount of added sugar while also boosting the levels of fibre and complex carbohydrates, so that these cakes take longer for the body to digest and give a more gradual energy boost.

Courgette, lime & chia

While courgettes may not seem like the most natural ingredient to add to a cake they add moistness, and when mixed with lime zest and juice, coconut and chia seeds they make a great-tasting cake that is high in unsaturated fats – the good guys. The icing is optional but adds a nice fresh tang.

1 Preheat the oven to 180°C/350°F/Gas 4. Cut a piece of baking parchment a little larger than an 18 x 28 x 4cm/7 x 11 x 1½in rectangular tin or pan, snip into the corners then press the paper into the tin so that base and sides are lined.

2 Add the oil, eggs, lime zest and juice to a bowl and whisk until smooth. Add the sugar, flour, desiccated coconut and chia seeds and mix together. Stir in the courgette.

3 Spoon into the prepared tin and spread into an even layer. Bake for 30–35 minutes until well risen and the top of the cake is firm when pressed. To test, insert a skewer into the centre, it should come out clean when the cake is ready.

4 Leave the cake to cool for 10 minutes then lift the cake and paper out of the tin and cool completely on a wire rack. Mix the icing sugar with the lime juice to make a thin icing then drizzle over the top of the cake. Sprinkle with the coconut flakes and the lime zest and leave to set for 30 minutes.

5 Cut into 16 bars and lift off the paper. Store in a plastic container in the refrigerator for up to 2 days.

NUTRITION TIP Cakes are traditionally made with butter which is full of saturated fats, but replacing with sunflower oil changes this to healthier unsaturated fat, and rather than creaming the butter and sugar together everything can be quickly stirred together instead. COOK'S TIP If you don't have a rectangular cake tin or pan the right size check the base measurement of your smallest roasting pan, chances are this will be the same size.

Dairy-free
Gluten-free

Cuts into 16
Prep: 25 mins
Cook: 30–35 mins

200ml/7fl oz/scant 1 cup sunflower oil

3 eggs

Grated zest of 2 limes

Juice of 1 lime

200g/7oz/generous 1 cup golden caster (superfine) sugar

225g/8oz/1½ cups gluten free self-raising (self-rising) flour

50g/2oz/½ cup unsweetened desiccated (dry shredded) coconut

2 tbsp/30ml chia seeds

175g/6oz/1 small courgette (zucchini), coarsely grated

To decorate (optional)

65g/2½oz/½ cup icing (confectioners') sugar, sifted

Juice of 1 lime

25g/1oz/⅓ cup coconut flakes

Grated zest of ½ lime

Energy 231kcal/968kJ; Protein 3.5g; Carbohydrate 28.4g, of which sugars 17.9g; Fat 12.2g, of which saturates 3.1g; Cholesterol 43mg; Calcium 72mg; Fibre 2.2g; Sodium 87mg.

Dairy-free
Gluten-free
Nut-free

Cuts into 20
Prep: 25 mins
Cook: 20–25 mins

100g/3¾oz gluten-free dark
(bittersweet) chocolate,
broken into pieces

75g/3oz/scant ½ cup soya
margarine

75g/3oz/6 tbsp light
muscovado (brown) sugar

25g/1oz/¼ cup unsweetened
cocoa powder

40g/1½oz/generous ⅓ cup
quinoa flakes

1 tsp/5ml gluten-free baking
powder

2 eggs, beaten

250g/9oz/2 medium bananas,
weighed with their skins on,
peeled and mashed

Few banana chips and
25g/1oz diced gluten-free
chocolate, to decorate
(optional)

Banana brownie squares

Chocolate brownies are always popular but can be loaded with sugar. This version replaces some of the sugar with naturally sweet bananas and is a great way to use up those that have gone a little soft in the fruit bowl, plus they are a good source of potassium which helps to regulate blood pressure.

1 Preheat the oven to 180°C/350°F/Gas 4. Cut a square of baking parchment a little larger than a 20cm/8in square shallow cake tin or pan, snip the paper diagonally into the corners then press the paper into the tin so that the base and sides are lined.

2 Melt the chocolate, margarine and sugar together in a bowl set over a pan of gently simmering water. Take off the heat and add the remaining ingredients (except those to decorate, if you wish), beat together until smooth then pour into the prepared tin.

3 Ease into an even layer, break the banana chips into slightly smaller pieces, if using, sprinkle over the top of the cake mixture then bake for 20–25 minutes until well risen and cracked around the edges with a slightly soft centre.

4 Scatter the diced chocolate, if you like, over the top and leave to cool in the tin for 10 minutes. Lift the brownies out of the tin holding the paper and transfer to a wire rack to cool completely.

5 Cut into 20 small squares and store in a plastic container in the refrigerator for up to 3 days.

NUTRITION TIP Adding quinoa flakes instead of flour boosts protein and makes these brownies gluten-free too.
COOK'S TIP Keep a watchful eye on the brownies while cooking, you want to catch them when the centre is still very slightly soft so that the cooled brownies have that lovely soft gooey texture.

Energy 101kcal/423kJ; Protein 1.7g; Carbohydrate 11.6g, of which sugars 9.7g; Fat 5.7g, of which saturates 1.8g; Cholesterol 23mg; Calcium 10mg; Fibre 0.7g; Sodium 47mg.

Clementine & almond squares

Dairy-free
Gluten-free

Cuts into 16
Prep: 25 mins
Cook: 65–70 mins

150g/5oz/2 clementine oranges, washed

225g/8oz/1 parsnip, peeled and diced

110g/4oz/½ cup golden caster (superfine) sugar

4 large (US extra large) eggs

100g/3¾oz/¾ cup ground almonds

25g/1oz/scant ¼ cup ground flaxseeds

1 tsp/5ml gluten-free baking powder

½ tsp/2.5ml almond extract

4 tbsp/60ml flaked (sliced) almonds, to decorate

Little icing (confectioners') sugar, sifted, to decorate (optional)

This rich moist cake is made by cooking whole clementine oranges in water then puréeing with naturally sweet parsnips and baking with ground almonds instead of flour, for a tangy almost marmalade-like flavour.

1 Add the clementine oranges to the base of a steamer, cover with water and bring to the boil. Set the steamer basket on top, add the parsnips, and cover and steam for 20 minutes until the parsnips are soft. Cook the clementines for another 10 minutes or so until they are also soft. Cool.

2 Preheat the oven to 180°C/350°F/Gas 4. Cut a piece of baking parchment a little larger than a 20cm/8in shallow square tin or pan, snip diagonally into the corners then press into the tin so that the base and sides are lined with paper.

3 Drain the clementines, quarter and add to a food processor with the parsnips. Blend until smooth.

4 Add the sugar and eggs and beat again until smooth. Add the ground almonds, flaxseeds, baking powder and almond extract and beat again briefly until smooth.

5 Spoon the cake mixture into the tin, spread into an even layer then sprinkle with the flaked almonds. Bake for 35–40 minutes until well risen and the flaked almonds are golden brown. Check after 20 minutes and cover the top of the cake loosely with foil if the flaked almonds seem to be over-browning.

6 Lift the cake out of the tin and cool on a wire rack. Dust the top lightly with sifted icing sugar, if liked. Cut into small squares, lift off the paper and store in a plastic container for up to 3 days in the refrigerator.

NUTRITION NOTE Cooking the whole orange means that you not only have maximum flavour but none of the fibre is lost.

Energy 131kcal/549kJ; Protein 4.7g; Carbohydrate 11g, of which sugars 9.3g; Fat 7.9g, of which saturates 1g; Cholesterol 58mg; Calcium 43mg; Fibre 1.6g; Sodium 29mg.

Mini blueberry & orange loaves

**Dairy-free
Nut-free**

Makes 8
Prep: 20 mins
Cook: 25 mins

350g/12oz/3 cups self-raising
(self-rising) flour

75g/3oz/generous ⅓ cup
caster (superfine) sugar

Finely grated zest of
2 medium oranges and
150ml/¼ pint/⅔ cup juice

3 eggs, beaten

75g/3oz/scant ½ cup soya
margarine, melted

200g/7oz/1⅓ cup blueberries

This reduced-sugar cake is just bursting with fresh blueberries; although they naturally contain sugar they are also high in vitamin C which helps boost the immune system. Foods that only contain sugar with no other intrinsic value are the real baddies.

1 Preheat the oven to 180°C/350°F/Gas 4. Lightly oil 8 mini loaf tins or pans that are 5 x 10 x 3cm/2 x 4 x 1in and line the base and two long sides of each with a strip of baking parchment.

2 Mix the flour and sugar together in a bowl. Add the orange zest and juice, eggs and melted margarine and whisk together with a fork until just mixed. Add the blueberries and mix briefly.

3 Divide the mixture between the mini tins and bake for 25 minutes until well risen and slightly cracked on top. To check insert a skewer into the centre of one of the cakes, when removed it should be clean.

4 Leave the cakes to cool for 10 minutes then loosen and turn out on to a wire rack to cool. Wrap individually in extra baking parchment and keep in a plastic container in the refrigerator for up to 3 days.

NUTRITION TIP Superfood blueberries contain anthocyanins, a cancer-fighting antioxidant that gives them their rich deep colour. They are also packed with vitamins C and K plus the mineral manganese.

COOK'S TIP If you are not on a dairy-free diet, then swap the soya margarine for butter. You might also like to use disposable card mini loaf cases, found in larger supermarkets or online.

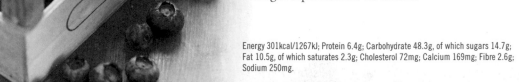

Energy 301kcal/1267kJ; Protein 6.4g; Carbohydrate 48.3g, of which sugars 14.7g; Fat 10.5g, of which saturates 2.3g; Cholesterol 72mg; Calcium 169mg; Fibre 2.6g; Sodium 250mg.

Green tea fruitcake squares

Chances are your granny would have made a version of this cake in a loaf tin with leftover tea from the teapot; while you can still do this, teabread gets a more modern makeover with green tea and naturally-sweet dried fruits with just a tiny amount of added sugar and a sticky marmalade glaze.

1 Add the fruit to a bowl, pour over the hot tea, cover and leave to soak for 4 hours or overnight.

2 Preheat the oven to 160°C/325°F/Gas 3. Cut a piece of baking parchment a little larger than a 20cm/8in shallow square cake tin or pan, snip into the corners then press the paper into the tin so that the base and sides are lined.

3 Add the flour to a larger bowl and stir in the sugar. Add the apple and citrus zest then the soaked fruit and any remaining tea in the bottom of the bowl. Stir together until well mixed.

4 Spoon into the tin, spread level and bake for 50–55 minutes until browned on top and firm to the touch. To test insert a skewer into the centre, it will come out clean when the cake is ready.

5 Leave the cake to cool for 20 minutes in the tin then loosen the edge, lift the cake out by the paper and put on to a wire rack, spread the top with the marmalade and leave to cool.

6 Cut the cake into bars then pack into a plastic container, interleaving with extra baking parchment. Cut into squares when needed. Store for up to 1 week.

COOK'S TIP As this cake is packed with fruit it almost improves with keeping. You might like to wrap one of the strips of cake, label and freeze for another time.

Dairy-free
Vegan
Nut-free

Cuts into 20
Prep: 20 mins
Soak: 4 hours or overnight
Cook: 50–55 mins

450g/1lb/3 cups dried mixed fruit

300ml/½ pint/1¼ cups hot green tea, strained if needed

250g/9oz/2¼ cups wholemeal (whole-wheat) self-raising (self-rising) flour

75g/3oz/6 tbsp light muscovado (brown) sugar

1 dessert apple, cored and coarsely grated

Grated zest of ½ lemon

Grated zest of ½ orange

1 tbsp/15ml fine-cut orange marmalade, to glaze

Energy 115kcal/492kJ; Protein 2.1g; Carbohydrate 27.6g, of which sugars 19.9g; Fat 0.4g, of which saturates 0g; Cholesterol 0mg; Calcium 22mg; Fibre 2.2g; Sodium 11mg.

Sweet potato gingerbreads

Think of moist, dark gingerbread and you tend to think of masses of sugar, syrup and treacle. This healthier version cuts the sugar with naturally-sweet roasted sweet potato and adds malted barley instead of syrup. Just like the bonfire party favourite, parkin, this recipe adds cholesterol-lowering oatmeal in place of some of the flour.

1 Preheat the oven to 180°C/350°F/Gas 4. Prick the sweet potatoes with a fork, put on to a baking sheet and bake for 40–45 minutes until soft when squeezed. Cool then cut into halves, scoop the potato flesh out of the skins and mash on a plate with a fork.

2 Lightly brush 10 individual loaf tins or pans 5 x 10 x 3cm/2 x 4 x 1in with a little oil then line the base and two long sides of each with a piece of baking parchment. Stand the tins on a baking sheet.

3 Add the margarine, sugar, malt extract and milk to a medium pan. Heat gently until the sugar has just dissolved then take off the heat and mix well. Mix in the eggs then all the dry ingredients, except the porridge oats, until smooth.

4 Divide between the loaf tins, spread the tops level and sprinkle with the oats, if liked. Bake for 20–25 minutes until well risen and a skewer comes out cleanly when inserted into one of the cakes.

5 Leave the cakes to cool in the tins for 10 minutes then loosen the edges, turn out and cool completely on a wire rack. Pack into a plastic container and eat within 3 days.

NUTRITION NOTE Barley malt extract is a thick treacle-like syrup that is a by-product of the brewing industry and used to be given to children in the post-war years as a dietary supplement mixed with cod liver oil; now it is more commonly added to artisan breads for its flavour and natural sweetness. It contains B vitamins.

Dairy-free

Makes 10
Prep: 25 mins
Cook: 60–70 mins

350g/12oz/2 small sweet potatoes, scrubbed

100g/3¾oz/scant ½ cup soya margarine

150g/5oz/generous ½ cup light muscovado (brown) sugar

75g/3oz/3 tbsp barley malt extract

125ml/4fl oz/½ cup unsweetened almond milk

2 eggs, beaten

100g/3¾oz/¾ cup medium oatmeal

110g/4oz/1 cup white spelt flour

2 tsp/10ml ground ginger

1 tsp/5ml ground mixed (apple pie) spice

½ tsp/2.5ml ground turmeric

1 tsp/5ml bicarbonate of soda (baking soda)

2 tbsp/30ml porridge (rolled) oats, to decorate (optional)

Energy 261kcal/1098kJ; Protein 4.4g; Carbohydrate 38.9g, of which sugars 17.6g; Fat 10.9g, of which saturates 2.1g; Cholesterol 46mg; Calcium 81mg; Fibre 2.6g; Sodium 125mg.

Chocolate beetroot cake

Rich, dark and very chocolately, this cake is made without dairy products, eggs or wheat so no-one need miss out.

1 Preheat the oven to 180°C/350°F/Gas 4. Cut a piece of baking parchment a little larger than a 20 x 30cm/8 x 12in Swiss roll tin or jelly roll pan, snip diagonally into the corners then press the paper into the tin so that the base and sides are lined and the paper stands a little above the sides of the tin.

2 Add the beetroot and milk to a pan, bring to the boil then simmer for 4–5 minutes until tender. Take off the heat and stir in the coconut oil then leave to cool.

3 Add the beetroot mix to a food processor with the vanilla and purée until smooth. Add the ground almonds, cocoa, sugar, flour and baking powder and blitz again until smooth. If you don't have a food processor blend the beetroot mix in a liquidizer then add to a bowl of the dry ingredients and stir.

4 Spoon into the prepared tin, level the surface and bake for 25 minutes until firm to the touch. Leave to cool in the tin. When cold, lift out of the tin and peel off the paper. Cut the cake in half through the long side to give 2 smaller even-sized rectangles.

5 To make the frosting, warm the coconut oil in a small pan until just melted. Stir in the cocoa, maple syrup and vanilla and mix until smooth and glossy. Transfer to a food processor or liquidizer with the avocado and beat until smooth. Spread half the frosting over one of the cake halves, top with the second cake then spread the remaining frosting on top.

6 Decorate with a few chopped goji berries, if liked. Leave the icing to set for 30 minutes and then cut into 12 small squares. Pack into a container and store in the refrigerator for 3 days.

Vegan
Gluten-free
Dairy-free

Cuts into 12
Prep: 25 mins
Cook: 25 mins

200g/7oz/2 trimmed beetroot (beets), peeled and diced
250ml/8fl oz/1 cup unsweetened almond milk
3 tbsp/45ml coconut oil
1½ tsp/7.5ml vanilla extract
75g/3oz/¾ cup ground almonds
75g/3oz/¾ cup unsweetened cocoa powder
150g/5oz/generous 1 cup light muscovado (brown) sugar
150g/5oz/1 cup gluten-free self-raising (self-rising) flour
1 tsp/5ml gluten-free baking powder

To decorate
2 tbsp/30ml coconut oil
3 tbsp/45ml unsweetened cocoa powder
2 tbsp/30ml maple syrup
½ tsp/2.5ml vanilla extract
1 large avocado, halved, stoned (pitted) and skinned
Few goji berries, roughly chopped (optional)

Energy 182kcal/764kJ; Protein 4g; Carbohydrate 25g, of which sugars 14.7g; Fat 8g, of which saturates 3.5g; Cholesterol 0mg; Calcium 74mg; Fibre 2.1g; Sodium 131mg.

Plum crumble squares

Gluten-free
Dairy-free

Cuts into 20
Prep: 25 mins
Cook: 45–50 mins

For the crumble topping
25g/1oz/¼ cup gluten-free
self-raising (self-rising) flour
25g/1oz/¼ cup demerara (raw)
sugar
25g/1oz/2 tbsp soya margarine
25g/1oz/3 tbsp sunflower
seeds
25g/1oz/3 tbsp pumpkin seeds

For the cake
110g/4oz/½ cup soya
margarine
110g/4oz/½ cup light
muscovado (brown) sugar
2 eggs, beaten
150g/5oz/1¼ cups gluten-free
self-raising (self-rising) flour
1 tsp/5ml vanilla extract
250g/9oz/5 small red plums,
halved, stoned (pitted) and
sliced

Cakes needn't be off the menu because you are trying to eat healthily, just opt for those that have reduced amounts of sugar and added nutrient-boosters such as seeds, fruit, vegetables or nuts.

1 Preheat the oven to 180°C/350°F/Gas 4. Cut a piece of baking parchment a little larger than a 20cm/8in shallow square cake tin or pan, snip into the corners then press the paper into the tin so that the base and sides are lined.

2 To make the crumble topping, add the flour, sugar and margarine to a small bowl and rub in with fingertips until the mixture looks like breadcrumbs. Stir in the seeds.

3 To make the cake, cream the margarine and sugar together in a bowl until light and fluffy. Gradually beat in the eggs and flour alternately until both have been added and the mixture is smooth.

4 Stir in the vanilla then spoon into the lined tin. Spread the top level then scatter the plums randomly over the top. Sprinkle with the crumble mix then bake for 45–50 minutes until well risen, the top of the cake is golden and a skewer comes out cleanly when inserted into the centre of the cake.

5 Leave to cool in the tin. Lift the cake and paper out of the tin, cut into 20 small squares, lift off the paper and pack into a plastic container. Store in the refrigerator for up to 3 days.

NUTRITION TIP Pumpkin seeds add iron and magnesium for maintaining healthy blood cells and zinc for normal growth and development while sunflower seeds are a useful source of vitamin E and are high in linoleic acid, needed for maintenance of cell membranes.

Energy 132kcal/553kJ; Protein 2.2g; Carbohydrate 14.8g, of which sugars 8.1g; Fat 7.5g, of which saturates 1.5g; Cholesterol 23mg; Calcium 10mg; Fibre 1g; Sodium 58mg.

Dairy-free
Gluten-free
Nut-free

Cuts into 20
Prep: 20 mins
Cook: 40 mins

110g/4oz/¾ cup prunes, pitted and chopped

110g/4oz/¾ cup dried dates, stoned (pitted) and chopped

25g/1oz piece fresh root ginger, peeled and finely chopped

2 tsp/5ml ground ginger

200ml/7fl oz/scant 1 cup unsweetened soya milk

75g/3oz/6 tbsp soya margarine

100g/3¾oz/½ cup dark muscovado (molasses) sugar

2 eggs, beaten

175g/6oz/1½ cups gluten-free self-raising (self-rising) flour

1 tsp/5ml gluten-free baking powder

2 tbsp/30ml sunflower seeds

2 tbsp/30ml pumpkin seeds

50g/2oz gluten-free dark (bittersweet) chocolate, melted

Sticky date, prune & ginger squares

Think sticky toffee pudding but as cake squares. This healthier version contains high-fibre prunes as well as naturally-sweet dates. Delicious served with a drizzle of dark chocolate on top.

1 Preheat the oven to 160°C/325°F/Gas 3. Cut a piece of baking parchment a little larger than an 18 x 28 x 4cm/ 7 x 11 x 1½in rectangular cake tin or pan, snip into the corners then press the paper into the tin so that the base and sides are lined.

2 Add the prunes, dates, fresh and ground ginger to a medium pan, add the soya milk and cook gently for about 5 minutes until the dried fruit is soft. Take off the heat and beat well. Cool for 10 minutes.

3 Cream the margarine and sugar together until light and fluffy with an electric whisk or food processor if you have one. Beat in a little of the egg then a little of the flour until all the egg has been added. Mix the baking powder into the remaining flour then beat into the cake mixture until smooth.

4 Add the fruit mix and beat again until smooth. Spoon into the prepared tin, spread the top level and sprinkle with the seeds. Bake for about 40 minutes until well risen and the top springs back when pressed with a fingertip. Leave to cool for 10 minutes then lift the cake on the paper on to a wire rack and leave to cool completely.

5 Drizzle the melted chocolate over the top of the cake. Leave to set for 10 minutes then cut into 20 small squares. Lift off the paper and pack into a plastic container, interleaving the layers with more paper. Press or clip on the lid and store in the refrigerator for up to 3 days.

Energy 122kcal/512kJ; Protein 2.9g; Carbohydrate 14.6g, of which sugars 7.6g; Fat 6.2g, of which saturates 1.5g; Cholesterol 23mg; Calcium 43mg; Fibre 1.5g; Sodium 70mg.

Spiced apple & carrot bites

All the flavour of this favourite cake but made with grated apple in place of the usual large amounts of sugar. Topped here with low-fat cream cheese frosting flavoured with a little vanilla and maple syrup, but it is just as tasty served plain.

1 Preheat the oven to 180°C/350°F/Gas 4. Cut a piece of baking parchment a little larger than an 18 x 28 x 4cm/7 x 11 x 1½in shallow baking tin or small roasting pan. Snip the paper into the corners then press the paper into the tin so that the base and sides are lined.

2 Add the eggs and oil to a mixing bowl and whisk together with a fork until mixed. Add the sugar, flour, spice and vanilla and mix with a fork until smooth then beat in the apple and carrots.

3 Spoon into the prepared tin, level the surface and bake for 35–40 minutes until well risen, golden brown and the top feels firm when pressed with a fingertip. Leave to cool in the tin for 10 minutes then transfer to a wire rack to cool completely.

4 For the frosting, beat the cream cheese with the maple syrup and vanilla. Peel the lining paper off the cake. Spread the frosting over the top and cut into 18 squares. Sprinkle each square with a little extra spice and top with a dried apple slice, if using. Store in a plastic container in the refrigerator for up to 2 days.

NUTRITION TIP Carrots are rich in beta-carotene, a powerful antioxidant which is converted in the body into vitamin A which aids eye-health, nourishes the skin and helps to fight the signs of ageing.

**Dairy-free
Nut-free**

Cuts into 18
Prep: 30 mins
Cook: 35–40 mins

3 eggs

150ml/¼ pint/⅔ cup light olive oil

150g/5oz/generous ½ cup light muscovado (brown) sugar

200g/7oz/1¾ cups self-raising (self-rising) wholemeal (whole-wheat) flour

2 tsp/10ml ground mixed (apple pie) spice

1 tsp/5ml vanilla extract

1 dessert apple, cored and coarsely grated

175g/6oz/2 medium carrots, peeled and coarsely grated

For the frosting

200g/7oz/scant 1 cup low-fat cream cheese

2 tsp/10ml maple syrup

1 tsp/5ml vanilla extract

A little extra ground spice or dried apple slices, see p60, to decorate (optional)

Energy 137kcal/582kJ; Protein 4.5g; Carbohydrate 26.3g, of which sugars 19.4g; Fat 2.3g, of which saturates 0.9g; Cholesterol 41mg; Calcium 31mg; Fibre 1.7g; Sodium 68mg.

Index